Family Matters: Navigating the Intersection of Family & Health Law

Welcome to "Family Matters: Navigating the Intersection of Family & Health Law." This book is a comprehensive exploration of the complex and often intertwined legal landscapes of family and health. In our fast-paced and ever-changing world, the intersection of family and health law has become increasingly significant, impacting the lives of individuals and families in profound ways.

Family law deals with the fundamental aspects of human relationships, such as marriage, divorce, child custody, adoption, and domestic partnerships. On the other hand, health law governs the rights and responsibilities related to healthcare, medical treatment, patient privacy, and the ethical considerations surrounding medical decision-making.

Within the pages of this book, we will delve into the myriad issues that arise at the crossroads of family and health law. From the legal complexities surrounding assisted reproductive technologies to the delicate balance of caring for elderly family members with dignity and respect, each chapter will illuminate the multifaceted dimensions of this dynamic field.

The dynamics of modern families have evolved, giving rise to new challenges and opportunities within the legal landscape. As societal norms shift, so do the legal frameworks that guide and protect families and individuals. Moreover, advances in medical science and technology have opened up novel ethical dilemmas,

1

influencing the way we approach health-related legal matters.

Throughout this journey, we will explore how family and health law intersect, intertwining to shape individual well-being and family structures. We will analyze landmark court cases that have redefined family dynamics and medical decision-making, and we will delve into the ethical dilemmas that arise when personal beliefs clash with medical necessity.

As we traverse this path, it becomes evident that family and health law are not isolated realms but interconnected forces that profoundly impact one another. Decisions made in family law can have far-reaching implications for an individual's healthcare choices, and vice versa.

At the heart of this exploration lies the recognition that the well-being of individuals and families is intricately linked to their access to quality healthcare and their legal rights within family dynamics. By gaining a comprehensive understanding of the complexities of family and health law, we empower ourselves to navigate these legal landscapes with knowledge and insight.

"Family Matters: Navigating the Intersection of Family & Health Law" is an invitation to explore the intricate dance between two domains of law that are deeply intertwined with the fabric of human life. It is a call to appreciate the challenges, complexities, and triumphs that individuals and families encounter in their pursuit of well-being and legal protection.

We embark on this journey with the hope that this book will serve as a valuable resource for legal professionals, students, policymakers, and individuals seeking a deeper understanding of the critical issues surrounding family and health law. Together, let us navigate the intersection of family and health, seeking to protect and promote the rights, health, and happiness of all those we encounter on this path.

I. Introduction

- The significance of family and health law intersection
- Overview of the book's objectives and scope

II. Family Law: Foundations and Modern Dynamics

- Definition and scope of family law
- Marriage, divorce, and legal partnerships
- Child custody and support
- Adoption and surrogacy
- Family law and LGBTQ+ rights

III. Health Law: Protecting Healthcare Rights and Ethics

- Understanding health law and its scope
- Patient rights and medical decision-making
- Informed consent and medical treatment
- Medical privacy and confidentiality
- Medical malpractice and liability

IV. Assisted Reproductive Technologies and Family Law

- Legal implications of assisted reproduction
- Surrogacy agreements and parental rights
- Donor conception and legal parentage
- Ethical considerations in reproductive technologies

V. Family and Health in Elder Care

- Legal issues in elder care and guardianship
- Advance directives and end-of-life decisions
- Long-term care planning and financing
- Elder abuse and protective measures

VI. Mental Health and Family Law

- Mental health considerations in family law disputes
- Involuntary commitment and legal rights
- Mental health and child custody evaluations
- Balancing privacy and intervention for mental health concerns

VII. Child Welfare and Family Law

- Child protection services and legal interventions
- Termination of parental rights and adoption
- Foster care and kinship care arrangements
- The role of family law in ensuring child well-being

VIII. Medical Decision-Making for Minors

- Consent and treatment decisions for minors
- Emancipated minors and medical autonomy
- Parental rights and medical decision-making conflicts
- Legal aspects of medical treatment for minors

IX. Ethics and Legal Challenges in End-of-Life Care

- Physician-assisted dying and right to die
- Advance healthcare directives and living wills
- Hospice and palliative care legal considerations
- The role of family law in end-of-life decisions

X. Genetics, Technology, and Family Law

- Legal implications of genetic testing and screening
- Preimplantation genetic diagnosis and legalities
- Genetic information and family law disputes
- Ethical dilemmas in genetic technologies

XI. Family Law and Public Health Emergencies

- Family law during pandemics and health crises
- Parental rights and health emergency decisions
- Medical treatment and consent during emergencies
- Legal aspects of quarantine and isolation measures

XII. Ethical Dilemmas at the Family and Health Law Intersection

- Balancing autonomy and protection in health decisions
- Confidentiality and disclosure in family health matters
- Cultural and religious beliefs versus medical necessities
- Addressing ethical dilemmas through legal frameworks

XIII. Future Perspectives on Family & Health Law

- Emerging challenges and opportunities
- Technological advancements and legal implications
- Integrating family and health law reforms
- Vision for a harmonious future at the intersection

XIV. Conclusion

- Recapitulation of key insights and themes discussed in the book
- A call to action for promoting a just and compassionate family and health law system

The significance of family and health law intersection

The intersection of family and health law holds immense significance as it addresses the delicate balance between personal relationships, individual well-being, and the complex healthcare landscape. Family law governs the fundamental aspects of human relationships, such as marriage, divorce, child custody, and adoption. Health law, on the other hand, regulates healthcare rights, medical decision-making, and ethical considerations in medical treatment.

The convergence of family and health law becomes particularly crucial during life-altering events, such as major health crises, end-of-life decisions, and assisted reproductive technologies. Family dynamics often play a pivotal role in medical decision-making, as close family members are often the primary caregivers and decision-makers for their loved ones' health needs.

For instance, during a medical crisis, family members may face difficult choices regarding the best treatment options, respecting the wishes of a patient, and ensuring that decisions align with legal and ethical standards. The legal frameworks surrounding medical consent, end-of-life care, and the rights of minors become integral in safeguarding both the health and family dynamics.

Furthermore, the emergence of medical technologies and genetic advancements raises intricate ethical questions related to assisted reproduction, genetic testing, and the impact on family structures. The legalities surrounding parental rights, custody, and the use of genetic information become crucial in ensuring a just and equitable family and health system.

Family and health law intersection also becomes relevant in matters of mental health care, elder care, and child welfare, where legal protections are necessary to ensure the well-being of vulnerable individuals within the family unit.

Moreover, the COVID-19 pandemic and other health crises have highlighted the need for legal measures to balance public health requirements and the rights of families during emergencies. Legal frameworks must navigate the complexities of quarantine, isolation measures, and medical consent in unprecedented times.

In summary, the significance of family and health law intersection lies in its capacity to protect individual rights, foster family well-being, and promote ethical medical practices. This intersection enables society to address the diverse needs and challenges of families while upholding the fundamental values of compassion, autonomy, and justice in the realm of healthcare and personal relationships.

Overview of the book's objectives and scope

"Family Matters: Navigating the Intersection of Family & Health Law" aims to provide a comprehensive and in-depth exploration of the complex legal landscapes where family dynamics intersect with health-related matters. The book seeks to shed light on the multifaceted dimensions of this dynamic field, examining the critical issues, challenges, and ethical dilemmas that arise at the crossroads of family and health law.

The primary objectives of the book are as follows:

1. Understanding the Interplay: The book endeavors to elucidate the intricate relationship between family law and health law. It explores how decisions made within one realm can significantly impact the other, and how individuals' health and well-being are intertwined with their family dynamics.

2. Analyzing Legal Frameworks: With a focus on legal frameworks and regulations, the book delves into the rights and responsibilities that govern family relationships and healthcare. It seeks to offer a clear understanding of the legal mechanisms designed to protect and guide families through various health-related situations.

3. Ethical Considerations: The book highlights the ethical dilemmas that arise at the intersection of family and health law, encouraging a thoughtful exploration of moral complexities. It provides insights into how legal frameworks address these dilemmas while balancing the principles of autonomy, beneficence, and justice.

4. Contemporary Issues: Recognizing the evolving nature

of family and health dynamics, the book addresses current and emerging issues, such as assisted reproductive technologies, mental health care, and genetics. It examines the legal and ethical implications of these advancements in the context of family life and health outcomes.

5. Promoting Well-Being: The book aims to promote the well-being of individuals and families by equipping readers with the knowledge and insights needed to navigate the legal complexities surrounding family and health matters. It seeks to empower legal professionals, policymakers, and individuals in making informed decisions that prioritize the best interests of all parties involved.

The scope of the book is comprehensive and encompassing. It covers various aspects of family law, such as marriage, divorce, child custody, adoption, and LGBTQ+ rights, while also exploring health law topics, including patient rights, medical decision-making, medical privacy, and malpractice. Additionally, the book delves into specific areas where family and health law intersect, such as assisted reproductive technologies, elder care, child welfare, and mental health care.

Furthermore, the book extends its reach to consider the impact of health crises and public health emergencies on family dynamics and the legal measures in place to address these challenges. It also delves into the ethical considerations and rights of individuals in medical emergencies and end-of-life decisions.

Throughout the journey, the book emphasizes the significance of public participation, inclusivity, and ethical considerations in shaping family and health law policies. It encourages readers to reflect on the call to action for a more compassionate, just, and sustainable family and health law system.

In essence, "Family Matters: Navigating the Intersection of Family

& Health Law" is a comprehensive guide and resource for legal professionals, students, policymakers, and individuals seeking a deeper understanding of the critical issues surrounding the confluence of family dynamics and health-related legal matters.

Definition and scope of family law

Family law is a branch of law that deals with legal matters pertaining to family relationships and domestic issues. It encompasses a wide range of legal issues that arise within families and governs the rights, responsibilities, and obligations of family members. The scope of family law includes various areas, such as marriage, divorce, child custody, child support, adoption, domestic violence, property division, and other related matters.

Family law is essential in providing legal structures and mechanisms to address the complex and sensitive issues that arise within families. It aims to protect the rights and interests of individuals, especially children, and to ensure that families function harmoniously within the framework of the law.

The scope of family law may vary from one jurisdiction to another, as different countries or states may have specific laws and regulations that govern family-related matters. Family law attorneys play a crucial role in providing legal advice and representation to individuals and families facing these legal issues, ensuring that their rights are upheld and that their cases are resolved fairly and justly.

Marriage, divorce, and legal partnerships

Marriage, divorce, and legal partnerships are significant aspects of family law that govern the formation, dissolution, and recognition of relationships between individuals. Let's explore each of these areas in more detail:

1. Marriage: Marriage is a legal and social contract that establishes a formal and recognized relationship between two individuals, typically with the intention of forming a family unit. The requirements and regulations for marriage can vary depending on the jurisdiction, but it often involves obtaining a marriage license and having a ceremony performed by an authorized officiant.

Family law governs the legal aspects of marriage, including the rights and responsibilities of spouses, property rights, inheritance, and support obligations. It also addresses issues related to prenuptial agreements, which are contracts that outline the distribution of assets in the event of divorce or death.

2. Divorce: Divorce is the legal termination of a marriage or the dissolution of a marital union. Family law provides guidelines and procedures for obtaining a divorce, including grounds for divorce, division of property, spousal support (alimony), child custody, and child support.

The divorce process can be emotionally and financially challenging, and family law seeks to protect the rights of both parties involved and ensure a fair resolution of disputes.

Mediation and collaborative divorce are alternative methods that aim to promote amicable resolutions without resorting to adversarial court proceedings.

3. Legal Partnerships: Family law also addresses legal partnerships that are not necessarily traditional marriages. These may include domestic partnerships, civil unions, or registered partnerships, depending on the jurisdiction. These legal arrangements grant similar rights and responsibilities to the partners as in a marriage, but they may be available to same-sex couples or opposite-sex couples who choose not to marry.

Overall, family law plays a crucial role in regulating and protecting the rights and interests of individuals in various types of family relationships. It seeks to provide a framework for addressing disputes, ensuring fairness, and promoting the well-being of all family members involved.

Child custody and support

Child custody and support are vital aspects of family law that deal with the well-being and financial care of children when their parents separate or divorce. Let's explore each of these areas in more detail:

1. Child Custody: Child custody refers to the legal and practical arrangements for the care and upbringing of a child after the parents' separation or divorce. There are two primary types of child custody:

- Physical Custody: This determines where the child will live and with whom. In some cases, one parent may have sole physical custody, while in others, both parents may share joint physical custody, allowing the child to spend time with each parent.

- Legal Custody: This pertains to the decision-making authority for the child's upbringing, including matters related to education, healthcare, religion, and other significant life choices. Legal custody can also be sole or joint, depending on the court's determination of what is in the best interest of the child.

Child custody decisions are made with the child's best interests in mind, and courts consider factors such as the child's age, emotional well-being, relationship with each parent, and the ability of each parent to provide a stable and nurturing environment.

2. Child Support: Child support is the financial support provided by one parent to the custodial parent for the care and upbringing of the child. The non-custodial

parent typically pays child support to ensure that the child's basic needs, such as food, shelter, clothing, and education, are adequately met.

The amount of child support is usually determined by state guidelines, taking into account factors such as each parent's income, the number of children, and any specific needs the child may have. Child support is a legal obligation, and failure to comply with court-ordered child support payments can have legal consequences.

Child custody and support are highly sensitive matters, and family law courts strive to make decisions that prioritize the best interests of the child while ensuring that both parents remain involved in their child's life, even after separation or divorce. Mediation and collaborative law are often used to facilitate open communication and reach amicable agreements regarding custody and support arrangements. However, when necessary, family courts will make decisions in the best interest of the child.

Adoption and surrogacy

Adoption and surrogacy are two alternative family-building options that play significant roles in family law, allowing individuals or couples to become parents when they face challenges in conceiving a child naturally. Let's explore each of these processes:

1. Adoption: Adoption is the legal process through which an individual or a couple assumes the parental rights and responsibilities of a child, who is not biologically related to them. Adoption can occur through various avenues, including:

- Domestic Adoption: Involves adopting a child from within the same country as the adopting parents. This can be done through public or private adoption agencies or directly from birth parents.

- International Adoption: Involves adopting a child from a foreign country. This process requires compliance with both the laws of the adoptive country and the laws of the child's country of origin.

- Stepparent Adoption: Occurs when a stepparent legally adopts the biological child of their spouse, thereby assuming full parental rights and responsibilities.

Adoption laws vary by jurisdiction, and the process typically involves home studies, background checks, and legal procedures to finalize the adoption. Adoption is a lifelong commitment, and the welfare of the child is of utmost importance in the decision-making process.

2. Surrogacy: Surrogacy is a reproductive arrangement in

which a woman (the surrogate) carries and gives birth to a child on behalf of another person or couple (the intended parents). There are two primary types of surrogacy:

- Traditional Surrogacy: Involves the surrogate using her own egg and being artificially inseminated with the sperm of the intended father or a sperm donor.
- Gestational Surrogacy: Involves the use of in vitro fertilization (IVF) to create an embryo using the egg of the intended mother or a donor and the sperm of the intended father or a donor. The resulting embryo is then transferred to the surrogate's uterus.

Surrogacy agreements are complex and involve legal contracts outlining the rights and responsibilities of all parties involved. The laws related to surrogacy vary widely between countries and states, and it is essential for the intended parents and the surrogate to seek legal advice before proceeding with the surrogacy process.

Adoption and surrogacy provide meaningful ways for individuals and couples to expand their families and experience the joys of parenthood. However, due to the complexity of these processes, it is essential to seek guidance from legal professionals and adoption or surrogacy agencies to navigate the legal and emotional aspects involved in these life-changing decisions.

Family law and LGBTQ+ rights

Family law and LGBTQ+ rights have been intertwined in recent years as societies around the world continue to advance towards greater inclusivity and recognition of diverse family structures. LGBTQ+ rights movements have played a significant role in advocating for legal recognition and protection of same-sex relationships, parenting rights, and overall equality within family law.

Several key areas in family law have seen notable developments in relation to LGBTQ+ rights:

1. Marriage Equality: One of the most significant milestones in LGBTQ+ rights has been the recognition of same-sex marriage. Many countries have legalized same-sex marriage, allowing LGBTQ+ couples to enjoy the same legal rights and protections as opposite-sex couples when it comes to marriage, divorce, property division, spousal support, and child custody.

2. Adoption and Parental Rights: In many jurisdictions, LGBTQ+ individuals and couples now have the right to adopt children, either through individual or joint adoption processes. Additionally, legal parental recognition for same-sex partners who are not biological parents has gained acceptance through second-parent adoption or step-parent adoption proceedings.

3. Parentage and Surrogacy: The legal recognition of parental rights for LGBTQ+ individuals and couples in cases of assisted reproductive technologies, such as surrogacy and in vitro fertilization, has been a

significant focus of advocacy. Clarifying parentage and surrogacy laws helps ensure that children born through these methods have legal ties to their intended parents, regardless of their sexual orientation or gender identity.

4. Recognition of Non-Biological Parents: Family law has been evolving to recognize non-biological parents in LGBTQ+ families, acknowledging the roles of co-parents, non-biological parents, and de facto parents in the lives of children.

5. Protection Against Discrimination: Family law has increasingly included provisions to protect LGBTQ+ individuals and families from discrimination based on sexual orientation or gender identity. These protections aim to ensure that LGBTQ+ individuals can access family law services and benefits without fear of prejudice or bias.

Despite these advancements, there are still challenges and discrepancies in family law for LGBTQ+ individuals and families, particularly in jurisdictions where LGBTQ+ rights are not fully recognized. Legal professionals, advocates, and policymakers continue to work towards ensuring that family law remains inclusive, respectful, and protective of the rights and well-being of all individuals, regardless of their sexual orientation or gender identity.

As society progresses, the intersection between family law and LGBTQ+ rights will undoubtedly continue to evolve, reflecting the ongoing efforts to create more equitable and inclusive legal frameworks for all families.

Understanding health law and its scope

Health law, also known as healthcare law or medical law, is a specialized field of legal practice that deals with the legal rights, responsibilities, and regulations related to healthcare, medical practice, and public health. It encompasses a wide range of legal issues that arise in the healthcare industry, affecting patients, healthcare providers, healthcare organizations, and government entities.

The scope of health law is broad and continually evolving to keep up with the complex and dynamic nature of the healthcare system. Some of the key areas covered by health law include:

1. Patient Rights: Health law addresses the rights of patients to receive adequate and appropriate medical care, informed consent, privacy, confidentiality, and the right to make decisions about their own healthcare.
2. Medical Malpractice: Health law deals with medical negligence and liability, which may arise when healthcare providers fail to meet the standard of care, leading to harm or injury to patients.
3. Healthcare Regulation: Health law involves the regulation of healthcare providers, facilities, and services. This includes licensing, accreditation, and compliance with state and federal regulations.
4. Healthcare Finance: Health law touches on the financial aspects of healthcare, including health insurance, Medicare, Medicaid, and the Affordable Care Act (ACA). It also deals with reimbursement rates, billing practices, and fraud and abuse in healthcare billing.
5. Bioethics and Medical Research: Health law addresses

the ethical and legal implications of medical research involving human subjects, as well as the use of genetic information and emerging biotechnologies.

6. Public Health: Health law encompasses laws related to public health initiatives, disease control, vaccination requirements, and responses to public health emergencies.

7. End-of-Life Care: Health law addresses issues related to advance directives, living wills, and medical decisions at the end of life.

8. Healthcare Disparities: Health law is concerned with addressing disparities in healthcare access and quality among different population groups.

9. Health Information Privacy and Security: Health law deals with the protection and disclosure of personal health information, as governed by laws such as the Health Insurance Portability and Accountability Act (HIPAA).

10. Mental Health Law: Health law includes legal considerations related to mental health treatment, involuntary commitment, and patients' rights in mental health facilities.

11. Pharmaceuticals and Medical Devices: Health law covers regulations related to the approval, marketing, and use of pharmaceuticals and medical devices.

The field of health law is interdisciplinary, drawing on legal principles, medical ethics, and healthcare policies. Legal professionals specializing in health law work with healthcare providers, patients, government agencies, insurance companies, and other stakeholders to navigate the complexities of the healthcare system and ensure compliance with the law while promoting the best interests of patients and the public's health. As the healthcare landscape continues to evolve, health law will remain a critical area of legal practice that plays a vital role in shaping the future of healthcare delivery and policy.

Patient rights and medical decision-making

Patient rights and medical decision-making are critical aspects of health law that focus on protecting the autonomy and dignity of individuals seeking medical care. These rights empower patients to participate actively in their healthcare and make informed choices about their medical treatment.

Some key elements of patient rights and medical decision-making in health law include:

1. Informed Consent: Patients have the right to receive complete and understandable information about their medical condition, treatment options, potential risks and benefits, and alternative treatments. Informed consent ensures that patients can make decisions based on accurate and relevant information.

2. Right to Refuse Treatment: Patients have the right to refuse medical treatment, even if it is recommended by a healthcare provider. This right is especially important in cases of medical procedures that carry significant risks or are against the patient's personal or religious beliefs.

3. Confidentiality and Privacy: Health law protects the confidentiality of patient medical information and ensures that patient privacy is respected. Healthcare providers must maintain the confidentiality of patient records and can only disclose medical information with the patient's consent or as required by law.

4. Advance Directives: Advance directives, such as living wills and healthcare proxies, allow patients to express their medical treatment preferences in advance, especially in situations where they may be unable to

communicate their wishes.

5. Right to Access Medical Records: Patients have the right to access their medical records and request copies of their health information for review and control.

6. Shared Decision-Making: Health law encourages shared decision-making between patients and healthcare providers, fostering a collaborative approach to medical decision-making that considers the patient's values, preferences, and goals.

7. Right to Second Opinion: Patients have the right to seek a second opinion from another healthcare provider before making important medical decisions, especially in complex or serious medical conditions.

8. Pediatric Patient Rights: Health law also addresses the rights of pediatric patients, ensuring that their best interests are considered in medical decisions while taking into account their evolving capacity to make decisions as they grow older.

9. End-of-Life Decisions: Health law recognizes the right of patients to make decisions about end-of-life care, including the right to withhold or withdraw life-sustaining treatments in accordance with their wishes.

10. Mental Health Patient Rights: Health law includes protections for individuals receiving mental health treatment, ensuring that their rights are respected and that involuntary treatment is carried out in accordance with legal standards.

Patient rights and medical decision-making are essential components of patient-centered care, and they play a crucial role in fostering a trusting relationship between patients and healthcare providers. By upholding these rights, health law seeks to promote patient autonomy, dignity, and overall well-being in the healthcare system.

Informed consent and medical treatment

Informed consent is a fundamental principle in medical ethics and health law that ensures patients have the right to make informed decisions about their medical treatment. It is the process by which healthcare providers communicate relevant information to patients, enabling them to understand the nature of their medical condition, the proposed treatment or procedure, its potential risks and benefits, and any available alternative options. Informed consent empowers patients to actively participate in their healthcare decisions and make choices that align with their values and preferences.

Key components of informed consent include:

1. Voluntary Decision-Making: Informed consent must be obtained voluntarily, without coercion or undue influence. Patients should feel free to accept or decline the proposed treatment without fear of negative consequences.

2. Capacity to Consent: Patients must have the capacity to understand the information provided and make rational decisions. In cases where a patient lacks decision-making capacity (e.g., due to cognitive impairment or unconsciousness), informed consent may be obtained from a surrogate decision-maker or through advance directives.

3. Information Disclosure: Healthcare providers are responsible for disclosing relevant information to patients in a clear and understandable manner. This includes the nature of the medical condition, the purpose and details of the proposed treatment,

the potential risks and benefits, and any feasible alternatives.

4. Patient Understanding: Healthcare providers should ensure that patients comprehend the information provided. Patients have the right to ask questions, seek clarifications, and have complex medical information explained in a way they can understand.

5. Documentation: Informed consent is typically documented through a formal consent form signed by the patient or their legally authorized representative. The consent form should include details about the information provided, questions answered, and the patient's agreement to undergo the proposed treatment.

6. Consent Reversibility: Patients have the right to change their minds and withdraw their consent at any time before or during the medical procedure.

Informed consent is not just a legal requirement but a vital aspect of patient-centered care. It establishes a trusting relationship between patients and healthcare providers, fosters shared decision-making, and respects the autonomy and dignity of patients. Healthcare professionals have an ethical obligation to obtain informed consent before initiating any medical intervention, ensuring that patients are partners in their healthcare journey and receive treatments that align with their individual needs and values.

Medical privacy and confidentiality

Medical privacy and confidentiality are essential principles in healthcare that protect patients' sensitive and personal health information from unauthorized disclosure. They are crucial components of the doctor-patient relationship, fostering trust, ensuring patients' autonomy, and promoting open communication between patients and healthcare providers.

Key aspects of medical privacy and confidentiality include:

1. Privacy: Medical privacy refers to the right of patients to keep their health information private. It includes the right to control who can access their medical records, the conditions under which their information can be shared, and the right to be free from unnecessary intrusion into their personal health matters.

2. Confidentiality: Medical confidentiality is the duty of healthcare providers to keep patient information confidential and not disclose it to others without the patient's explicit consent or other legal justifications. This applies to all forms of communication, such as in-person conversations, medical records, electronic health records, and any other means of storing or transmitting patient information.

3. Protected Health Information (PHI): PHI includes any individually identifiable health information that is created, received, or maintained by a covered entity (e.g., healthcare providers, health plans) during the provision of healthcare services. This includes information such as patient names, addresses, medical history, and treatment plans.

4. HIPAA: The Health Insurance Portability and Accountability Act (HIPAA) is a federal law in the United States that establishes standards for protecting the privacy and security of PHI. HIPAA requires covered entities to implement administrative, physical, and technical safeguards to ensure the confidentiality of patient information.
5. Exceptions to Confidentiality: While healthcare providers are generally required to maintain patient confidentiality, there are specific situations where they may be legally obligated or permitted to disclose patient information without consent. These exceptions may include public health reporting, reporting of suspected abuse or neglect, court orders, and situations involving threats to public safety.
6. Breach Notification: In the event of a breach of medical privacy, healthcare providers must notify affected individuals and, in some cases, regulatory authorities, as required by law.

Medical privacy and confidentiality are foundational to ethical healthcare practices and are protected by law in many countries. Patients must feel confident that their personal health information will be kept secure and disclosed only when necessary for their care or with their explicit consent. Healthcare providers and institutions play a crucial role in upholding these principles and maintaining the trust of their patients.

Medical malpractice and liability

Medical malpractice refers to a situation in which a healthcare professional or healthcare facility deviates from the standard of care expected in their field, resulting in harm or injury to a patient. Medical malpractice can occur in various healthcare settings, including hospitals, clinics, private practices, and nursing homes.

Key aspects of medical malpractice and liability include:

1. Standard of Care: Medical malpractice is determined by comparing the actions of the healthcare provider to the standard of care expected of a reasonable and competent healthcare professional in similar circumstances. The standard of care is typically defined by the prevailing practices within the medical community.

2. Elements of Medical Malpractice: To prove medical malpractice, the injured party (plaintiff) must demonstrate the following elements: a. Existence of a doctor-patient relationship. b. Breach of the standard of care by the healthcare provider. c. Causation: Establishing a direct link between the breach of care and the patient's injury. d. Damages: The plaintiff must have suffered harm, such as physical injury, emotional distress, or financial losses, as a result of the healthcare provider's actions.

3. Types of Medical Malpractice: Medical malpractice can occur in various ways, including misdiagnosis or delayed diagnosis, surgical errors, medication errors, birth injuries, anesthesia errors, failure to obtain informed consent, and inadequate follow-up care.

4. Informed Consent: Healthcare providers are required to obtain informed consent from patients before performing any medical procedure or treatment. Informed consent means that patients have been adequately informed about the risks, benefits, and alternatives to the proposed treatment or procedure.

5. Liability and Insurance: Healthcare providers, including doctors, nurses, and other medical professionals, are required to carry malpractice insurance to protect themselves from potential liability in the event of a malpractice claim. Medical facilities and hospitals also typically carry liability insurance to cover potential claims against them.

6. Statute of Limitations: Medical malpractice claims are subject to statutes of limitations, which vary by jurisdiction. This means that there is a specific time limit within which a patient must file a malpractice lawsuit after discovering the injury.

7. Medical Review Panels: Some jurisdictions require medical malpractice cases to be reviewed by a panel of medical experts before proceeding to court. These panels assess the merits of the case and offer non-binding opinions on whether malpractice occurred.

Medical malpractice cases are complex and often require expert testimony from medical professionals in the same field. If a healthcare provider is found liable for malpractice, they may be required to compensate the injured patient for medical expenses, lost wages, pain and suffering, and other damages.

It is important for healthcare professionals to adhere to the standard of care and maintain open communication with patients to reduce the risk of malpractice claims. For patients, seeking legal advice from an experienced medical malpractice attorney is essential if they suspect they have been harmed due to medical negligence.

Legal implications of assisted reproduction

Assisted reproduction refers to the use of medical interventions and technologies to help individuals or couples conceive and have children. While these methods have provided hope and options for many aspiring parents, they also raise various legal and ethical considerations. Some of the key legal implications of assisted reproduction include:

1. Parental Rights: Assisted reproduction techniques, such as in vitro fertilization (IVF) and surrogacy, may involve multiple individuals in the process of conception and pregnancy. Determining legal parental rights and responsibilities can be complex, especially in cases involving sperm or egg donors, gestational carriers, or same-sex couples.

2. Surrogacy Agreements: Surrogacy involves a legal agreement between the intended parents and the surrogate. These agreements typically outline the rights, obligations, and compensation for the surrogate and intended parents. Laws regarding surrogacy vary widely by jurisdiction, and some countries or states have restrictions or outright bans on surrogacy.

3. Donor Agreements: In cases of using donated sperm, eggs, or embryos, legal agreements are often established to clarify the rights and obligations of the donor, recipient, and any resulting children. Donor anonymity and the use of known donors can also impact legal considerations.

4. Legal Parentage: In some cases, legal parentage may be established through traditional means, such as

adoption, even if the child is biologically related to one or both parents. Legal parentage may also be determined through court orders or birth certificates.

5. Consent and Informed Consent: Assisted reproduction procedures require informed consent from all parties involved, including the donors, recipients, and surrogates. Ensuring that all parties fully understand the potential risks, benefits, and legal implications is crucial.

6. Embryo Disposition: Decisions about the disposition of unused embryos created during IVF are important and may involve various legal considerations, including decisions about freezing, donation, destruction, or transfer to another party.

7. State and International Laws: Laws related to assisted reproduction vary significantly by country and even by state or province within a country. Some jurisdictions have comprehensive laws addressing assisted reproduction, while others have limited or no specific legislation.

8. Health Insurance Coverage: The availability of health insurance coverage for assisted reproductive procedures can vary widely. Some insurance policies may cover certain aspects of fertility treatments, while others may not.

9. Child Welfare and Protection: The best interests of the child are always a primary concern in cases involving assisted reproduction. Legal protections and rights of children born through these methods may differ from those of naturally conceived children.

10. Ethics and Personal Beliefs: Assisted reproduction raises ethical considerations that may be influenced by cultural, religious, or personal beliefs. Balancing these considerations with legal requirements can be challenging.

Navigating the legal implications of assisted reproduction requires careful planning, legal guidance, and a thorough understanding of the laws in the relevant jurisdiction. As the field of assisted reproduction continues to evolve, legal frameworks will need to adapt to protect the rights and interests of all parties involved.

Surrogacy agreements and parental rights

Surrogacy agreements are legally binding contracts that outline the terms and conditions of the surrogacy arrangement between the intended parents and the surrogate. These agreements are essential to clarify the rights and responsibilities of all parties involved and to protect everyone's interests throughout the surrogacy process.

In a surrogacy agreement, the following key aspects are typically addressed:

1. Intentions of the Parties: The agreement should clearly state the intentions of the intended parents and the surrogate, confirming that they are entering into the surrogacy arrangement voluntarily and with full understanding of its implications.
2. Compensation and Expenses: The agreement should specify the financial arrangements, including the compensation provided to the surrogate for carrying the pregnancy and any additional expenses related to the surrogacy, such as medical costs, legal fees, and travel expenses.
3. Medical Procedures and Treatments: Details about the medical procedures and treatments involved in the surrogacy process should be outlined, including the use of assisted reproductive technologies (e.g., in vitro fertilization) and prenatal care.
4. Parental Rights and Surrender of Custody: The agreement should address the intended parents' legal parentage rights and confirm that the surrogate intends to relinquish any parental rights and responsibilities

over the child.

5. Health and Lifestyle Requirements: The surrogate's health and lifestyle requirements, such as refraining from smoking or alcohol during pregnancy, adhering to prenatal care, and maintaining a healthy lifestyle, may be included in the agreement.

6. Birth Plan: The birth plan should be discussed and agreed upon, including the intended location of the birth and the intended parents' presence during delivery.

7. Confidentiality and Privacy: Both parties may agree to maintain confidentiality and privacy regarding the surrogacy arrangement, especially if the parties wish to keep the surrogacy private.

It is essential to consult with legal professionals experienced in family and reproductive law to draft a comprehensive and enforceable surrogacy agreement that complies with the laws of the relevant jurisdiction. The laws governing surrogacy agreements vary significantly by country and even within different states or provinces, so it is crucial to ensure compliance with local regulations.

Regarding parental rights, the legal process for establishing parental rights varies based on the jurisdiction and the type of surrogacy involved. In some cases, pre-birth orders or post-birth court orders may be required to legally recognize the intended parents as the child's legal parents. In other cases, the intended parents may need to go through an adoption process.

It is important for all parties involved in a surrogacy arrangement to understand and abide by the terms of the surrogacy agreement and to seek legal counsel to ensure that their rights and interests are protected throughout the process. Clear communication and a well-drafted surrogacy agreement are essential for a successful and harmonious surrogacy journey.

Donor conception and legal parentage

Donor conception involves using donated eggs, sperm, or embryos to help individuals or couples conceive a child. In cases of donor conception, legal parentage can be a complex and sensitive issue that varies depending on the laws of the country or state involved. It is crucial for all parties involved to understand their rights and responsibilities and to seek legal guidance to ensure compliance with applicable laws.

Legal parentage in donor conception can be determined through various means, including:

1. Consent and Agreements: In some jurisdictions, there may be specific legal requirements for obtaining the consent of all parties involved, including the donors, intended parents, and, if applicable, the surrogate. Written agreements may be used to outline the rights and responsibilities of each party.
2. Pre-Birth Orders: In some places, pre-birth orders may be obtained before the child's birth, establishing the intended parents as the legal parents of the child. These orders may be available to married or unmarried couples, same-sex couples, and single individuals using donor conception.
3. Post-Birth Legal Processes: In other cases, intended parents may need to go through legal procedures after the child's birth to establish their legal parentage. This could involve adoption or other court processes.
4. Same-Sex Parenting: In cases of same-sex couples using donor conception, legal parentage may be determined differently based on the laws of the jurisdiction. Some

places may have specific provisions recognizing same-sex parents as legal parents, while others may require additional legal steps.

5. Surrogacy Arrangements: In donor conception involving a surrogate, additional legal considerations may come into play. The intended parents' legal parentage may need to be established through a surrogacy agreement and court orders.

6. International Considerations: In cases involving international donor conception, where the intended parents, donors, or surrogates are from different countries, additional legal complexities may arise due to varying laws and regulations.

Given the complexity and variability of legal parentage in donor conception, it is essential for all parties involved to consult with legal professionals experienced in family and reproductive law. Legal counsel can provide guidance on the specific laws and procedures in their jurisdiction, ensure compliance with the legal requirements, and protect the rights and interests of all parties throughout the process.

Furthermore, open and honest communication between the intended parents, donors, and, if applicable, the surrogate is crucial in donor conception to establish clear expectations and ensure that everyone's rights and interests are respected and protected.

Ethical considerations in reproductive technologies

Ethical considerations in reproductive technologies are essential to address the complex moral dilemmas that arise from advances in the field of assisted reproductive technologies (ART). These technologies offer new possibilities for individuals and couples to conceive and have children, but they also raise ethical questions related to autonomy, justice, privacy, safety, and the well-being of the parties involved. Some of the key ethical considerations include:

1. Autonomy and Informed Consent: Individuals undergoing reproductive technologies should have the right to make informed decisions about their bodies and reproductive choices. Ensuring proper informed consent, respecting individual autonomy, and providing comprehensive information about risks and benefits are vital ethical principles.

2. Justice and Access: Access to reproductive technologies should be equitable and fair. Ethical concerns arise when there are disparities in access based on socioeconomic status, race, or other factors. Addressing these inequalities is crucial to promote justice in reproductive healthcare.

3. Welfare of the Child: The well-being of the child born through reproductive technologies is a central ethical consideration. Ensuring that children born through these technologies have the best possible start in life and that their rights and interests are protected is of utmost

importance.

4. Safety and Efficacy: Reproductive technologies must be subjected to rigorous scientific evaluation to ensure their safety and efficacy. Ethical concerns arise when unproven or experimental procedures are used without sufficient evidence of their effectiveness and safety.

5. Privacy and Confidentiality: Privacy and confidentiality of individuals involved in reproductive technologies, including donors, intended parents, and surrogates, should be protected. Respecting their privacy rights is crucial to maintaining trust and ensuring their emotional and psychological well-being.

6. Commercialization and Exploitation: Ethical concerns arise when reproductive technologies are commercialized and exploited for profit. Ensuring that financial considerations do not compromise the well-being and autonomy of the individuals involved is essential.

7. Multiple Gestation and Fetal Reduction: Reproductive technologies can lead to multiple pregnancies, which may carry risks for both the mother and the fetuses. The ethical question of fetal reduction arises when there are multiple embryos implanted, leading to the need to select and reduce the number of viable fetuses.

8. Parental Responsibilities and Rights: Ethical considerations extend to the rights and responsibilities of the intended parents, donors, and surrogates. Clarifying legal parentage, responsibilities, and rights is essential to prevent conflicts and ensure the well-being of the child.

9. Genetic Testing and Selection: The use of genetic testing and selection in reproductive technologies raises ethical questions about the potential for eugenics and discrimination. Ensuring that genetic testing is used responsibly and without promoting harmful practices is crucial.

To address these ethical considerations, it is essential for the medical community, policymakers, and society at large to engage in thoughtful and informed discussions. Guidelines and regulations should be established to promote ethical practices in reproductive technologies while respecting the rights and autonomy of the individuals involved and safeguarding the well-being of children born through these methods.

Legal issues in elder care and guardianship

Legal issues in elder care and guardianship are crucial to ensure the well-being and protection of elderly individuals who may be vulnerable due to age-related limitations or cognitive impairments. Some of the key legal issues in elder care and guardianship include:

1. Guardianship and Conservatorship: When an elderly individual is no longer capable of making decisions regarding their personal or financial matters, a court may appoint a guardian or conservator to act on their behalf. The guardian or conservator assumes the responsibility of making decisions in the best interest of the elderly person.

2. Advance Directives: Advance directives, such as living wills and durable power of attorney for healthcare, allow elderly individuals to express their healthcare preferences and designate someone to make medical decisions on their behalf if they become incapacitated.

3. Elder Abuse and Neglect: Legal protections against elder abuse and neglect are crucial to safeguard vulnerable elderly individuals from physical, emotional, or financial harm. Laws are in place to identify, prevent, and respond to instances of abuse or neglect.

4. Long-Term Care Planning: Legal issues related to long-term care planning involve financial planning to cover the costs of nursing home care, assisted living facilities, or in-home care. This may include understanding Medicaid and Medicare eligibility and asset protection strategies.

5. Healthcare Decision-Making: Ensuring that healthcare decisions for elderly individuals are made based on their wishes and best interests is an important legal consideration. This includes addressing issues of consent for medical treatment and end-of-life care.

6. Estate Planning: Elderly individuals may need to address estate planning matters, including wills, trusts, and the distribution of assets among beneficiaries. Proper estate planning can help avoid probate and ensure that their wishes are carried out after their passing.

7. Age Discrimination: Legal protections against age discrimination ensure that elderly individuals have equal access to employment, housing, and public services. Age discrimination laws also apply in healthcare settings.

8. Social Security and Pension Benefits: Understanding and navigating the complexities of social security benefits, pensions, and retirement plans are essential to secure financial stability during retirement.

9. Elder Financial Exploitation: Legal protections are in place to address instances of financial exploitation, fraud, or undue influence targeting elderly individuals, particularly those who may be vulnerable due to cognitive decline.

10. Nursing Home and Assisted Living Regulations: Legal regulations govern the operation and standards of nursing homes and assisted living facilities to protect the safety and well-being of elderly residents.

Addressing these legal issues requires a comprehensive and compassionate approach that considers the unique needs and circumstances of each elderly individual. Legal professionals, healthcare providers, and caregivers play a vital role in advocating for the rights and well-being of elderly individuals and ensuring that their interests are protected.

Advance directives and end-of-life decisions

Advance directives are legal documents that allow individuals to express their healthcare preferences and decisions in advance, especially for situations where they may become incapacitated or unable to communicate their wishes. These documents ensure that an individual's healthcare decisions align with their values, beliefs, and desires, even when they are no longer able to make those decisions themselves.

Key components of advance directives include:

1. Living Will: A living will is a written statement that specifies an individual's preferences for medical treatment and end-of-life care. It may address matters such as resuscitation, life support, pain management, and organ donation. Living wills are used to guide healthcare providers and family members in making medical decisions on behalf of the individual when they cannot communicate.
2. Durable Power of Attorney for Healthcare: This document designates a healthcare proxy or agent who is authorized to make medical decisions on behalf of the individual if they become unable to do so themselves. The appointed agent should be someone the individual trusts and understands their wishes for medical care.

End-of-life decisions often come into play when an individual is facing a terminal illness or a condition that leaves them in a permanent vegetative state. Advance directives provide clarity and relieve loved ones of the burden of making difficult medical decisions on behalf of the incapacitated person.

It is crucial for individuals to discuss their end-of-life preferences with their healthcare proxy, family members, and medical providers. Open communication ensures that everyone involved understands the individual's wishes and can carry them out in a manner consistent with their beliefs and values.

By having advance directives in place, individuals can have peace of mind knowing that their healthcare decisions will be respected and aligned with their personal choices, even when they are unable to advocate for themselves. It is recommended to review and update advance directives periodically or whenever there are significant changes in one's health or personal circumstances. Legal professionals can assist individuals in creating and properly executing advance directives to ensure that they are legally valid and enforceable.

Long-term care planning and financing

Long-term care planning involves preparing for the possibility of needing assistance with activities of daily living and medical care for an extended period, typically due to aging, chronic illness, or disability. It is a critical aspect of financial and estate planning, ensuring that individuals can receive the care they need while protecting their assets and preserving their quality of life. Here are some key considerations for long-term care planning and financing:

1. Assessing Care Needs: Begin by evaluating your current health status, family medical history, and lifestyle to estimate the potential need for long-term care. Consider factors such as age, existing medical conditions, and the availability of family support.

2. Understanding the Types of Long-Term Care: Long-term care can be provided in various settings, including nursing homes, assisted living facilities, home care, and adult day care centers. Each option has different costs and benefits, so it's essential to understand the available choices.

3. Long-Term Care Insurance: Long-term care insurance is a specialized insurance policy designed to cover the costs of extended care services. It can provide financial protection and help offset the expenses associated with long-term care, including nursing home care, home care, and assisted living facilities.

4. Self-Funding: Self-funding involves using personal savings, investments, or assets to pay for long-term care services. While it provides flexibility, it may deplete

resources if care needs are extensive and long-lasting.

5. Medicaid Planning: Medicaid is a joint federal and state program that provides financial assistance for long-term care to those with limited income and assets. Medicaid planning involves structuring assets and income to meet the eligibility requirements for Medicaid benefits while preserving assets for a spouse or family members.

6. Veterans Benefits: Veterans and their spouses may be eligible for certain long-term care benefits through the U.S. Department of Veterans Affairs (VA). These benefits can help cover the costs of nursing home care, assisted living, and home care services.

7. Long-Term Care Annuities: Long-term care annuities are financial products that provide a steady stream of income to cover long-term care expenses. They offer a combination of insurance and investment components.

8. Reverse Mortgages: A reverse mortgage allows homeowners aged 62 or older to convert a portion of their home equity into cash, which can be used to fund long-term care expenses.

9. Estate Planning: Incorporate long-term care planning into your overall estate planning, including the creation of a will, trust, and power of attorney documents.

Long-term care planning should be personalized to your specific needs and financial situation. Consulting with a financial advisor, elder law attorney, or insurance professional can help you navigate the complexities of long-term care planning and ensure that you have a comprehensive and well-designed strategy in place.

Elder abuse and protective measures

Elder abuse is a significant concern that affects many older adults around the world. It refers to any intentional or negligent act that causes harm or distress to an older person, often involving physical, emotional, financial, or sexual abuse, as well as neglect and exploitation. To protect older adults from abuse and ensure their safety and well-being, various measures and resources are available:

1. Education and Awareness: Raising awareness about elder abuse among older adults, their families, caregivers, and the community is crucial. Educational programs can help individuals recognize the signs of abuse and know how to report it.
2. Reporting Mechanisms: Establishing clear and accessible reporting mechanisms is essential to encourage individuals to report suspected cases of elder abuse. Hotlines, websites, and community resources can offer confidential reporting options.
3. Legal Protections: Laws and regulations should be in place to protect older adults from abuse and prosecute offenders. These laws may include enhanced penalties for elder abuse, mandatory reporting requirements for healthcare professionals, and safeguards against financial exploitation.
4. Guardianship and Conservatorship: In cases where older adults are unable to manage their affairs, appointing a trusted guardian or conservator can protect them from financial exploitation and ensure their best interests are upheld.

5. Adult Protective Services: Many countries have adult protective service agencies that investigate and address cases of elder abuse. These agencies work with law enforcement, social workers, and healthcare professionals to protect vulnerable older adults.

6. Healthcare and Social Services: Healthcare providers, social workers, and community organizations play a crucial role in identifying and addressing elder abuse. They can provide support, resources, and intervention for victims.

7. Financial Planning and Fraud Prevention: Older adults can protect themselves from financial exploitation by working with financial advisors to develop sound financial plans and be cautious about sharing personal information with others.

8. Supportive Services: Providing supportive services, such as home care, respite care, and senior centers, can help reduce the risk of elder abuse by ensuring that older adults have the assistance they need and opportunities for social engagement.

9. Empowering Older Adults: Encouraging older adults to be aware of their rights, assert their autonomy, and report any abuse they experience or witness is essential in preventing and addressing elder abuse.

10. Community Involvement: Engaging the community in efforts to prevent elder abuse can help create a supportive and protective environment for older adults.

It is crucial for individuals, families, caregivers, healthcare professionals, and policymakers to work together to prevent elder abuse and ensure the safety and dignity of older adults. By implementing these protective measures and promoting awareness, we can create a society that respects and safeguards the rights of older adults.

Mental health considerations in family law disputes

Mental health considerations play a significant role in family law disputes, as they can impact the well-being of all parties involved, including the children. When navigating family law matters such as divorce, child custody, visitation, and support, it is essential to address mental health issues with sensitivity and understanding. Here are some key considerations:

1. Child Custody and Parenting Arrangements: In child custody cases, the mental health of both parents is taken into account. Courts consider the ability of each parent to provide a stable and safe environment for the child. If one parent has mental health challenges, the court may assess their ability to care for the child and make decisions in their best interest.

2. Parental Fitness: In determining parental fitness, courts may consider the mental health of each parent, including their ability to care for the child's physical and emotional needs. A history of mental health treatment or past issues with mental health may be relevant in these assessments.

3. Court-Ordered Evaluations: In some cases, the court may order mental health evaluations of one or both parents to assess their ability to provide adequate care and support for the child. These evaluations may include psychological testing and interviews.

4. Substance Abuse and Mental Health: Substance abuse and mental health disorders often go hand in hand. In

family law cases, substance abuse issues, which may have underlying mental health causes, can significantly impact custody and visitation decisions.

5. Mental Health of Children: The mental health and well-being of children involved in family law disputes are of utmost importance. Courts may consider the child's mental health and any special needs or support required when making custody and visitation decisions.

6. Mediation and Counseling: In some cases, parties involved in family law disputes may benefit from mediation or counseling to address mental health issues and improve communication and cooperation.

7. Protective Orders: In situations involving domestic violence or mental health concerns that pose a risk to family members, courts may issue protective orders to safeguard the safety and well-being of those involved.

8. Co-Parenting and Communication: Effective co-parenting requires open and respectful communication between parents. Mental health challenges can impact communication, and parties may need support and guidance in maintaining a healthy co-parenting relationship.

9. Parental Rights and Termination: In extreme cases where parental mental health poses a significant risk to the child's safety and well-being, parental rights may be terminated.

10. Confidentiality and Privacy: Mental health information is sensitive and protected under confidentiality laws. Family law professionals must handle mental health information with discretion and respect for privacy.

Overall, addressing mental health considerations in family law disputes requires a multidimensional approach that prioritizes the well-being of all parties involved. By acknowledging and accommodating mental health challenges, the legal system can strive to reach fair and just outcomes that prioritize the best interests of the children and promote healthy family dynamics.

Involuntary commitment and legal rights

Involuntary commitment refers to the legal process through which a person is placed in a psychiatric hospital or treatment facility against their will. It is typically done when there are concerns about the person's mental health and safety, and it is believed that they may harm themselves or others if left untreated. Involuntary commitment is a serious matter and involves a delicate balance between protecting the individual's rights and ensuring their safety and well-being.

The process of involuntary commitment varies from country to country and state to state, but generally, it involves several key components:

1. Criteria for Involuntary Commitment: Most jurisdictions have specific criteria that must be met for someone to be involuntarily committed. These criteria usually involve evidence of a mental illness or disorder, the potential for harm to self or others, and the need for immediate treatment.
2. Emergency Detention: In some situations, when there is an immediate risk of harm, a person can be detained temporarily by law enforcement or mental health professionals for an emergency evaluation. This typically lasts for a short period (e.g., 24 to 72 hours) and allows for an assessment of the person's mental state.
3. Court Involvement: In many cases, a court hearing is required to authorize the involuntary commitment beyond the emergency detention period. The court will review evidence and testimony from mental health

professionals, the individual, and other relevant parties to determine if commitment is necessary.

4. Due Process and Legal Representation: Involuntary commitment proceedings must adhere to the principles of due process, including the right to legal representation. The individual has the right to present their case, challenge evidence, and have their rights protected throughout the process.

5. Periodic Review: Involuntary commitment is not indefinite. Laws often require regular reviews of the individual's status to assess if the commitment remains necessary or if less restrictive alternatives are appropriate.

6. Least Restrictive Treatment: The principle of "least restrictive treatment" is often applied in involuntary commitment cases. This means that authorities must consider less restrictive alternatives, such as outpatient treatment, before resorting to hospitalization.

7. Right to Appeal: In many jurisdictions, individuals who have been involuntarily committed have the right to appeal the decision and request a discharge from the psychiatric facility.

It is essential to balance the need to protect individuals and public safety with the respect for individual rights and dignity. Involuntary commitment is a serious step that should only be taken when there is clear evidence of a severe mental health crisis. Mental health professionals, legal authorities, and advocates work together to ensure that the process is fair, transparent, and focused on providing appropriate care and treatment to those in need.

Mental health and child custody evaluations

Mental health and child custody evaluations are conducted in the context of family law cases where there are concerns about the mental health of one or both parents and its potential impact on the well-being of the children involved. These evaluations aim to assess the mental health of the parents, their ability to provide a safe and stable environment for the child, and their capacity to meet the child's emotional, physical, and developmental needs.

Here are some key aspects of mental health and child custody evaluations:

1. Purpose: The primary purpose of these evaluations is to help the court make informed decisions about child custody and visitation arrangements that are in the best interests of the child. The evaluation aims to provide an objective assessment of the mental health of each parent and its potential impact on the child's safety and well-being.

2. Mental Health Professionals: The evaluation is typically conducted by mental health professionals, such as psychologists, psychiatrists, or social workers, who have expertise in child custody evaluations and family dynamics. These professionals are neutral and objective and focus on the well-being of the child.

3. Evaluation Process: The evaluation process often involves a series of interviews, observations, and psychological assessments of each parent. The evaluator may also interview the child and other relevant individuals, such as teachers or caregivers. The evaluation may take several sessions to complete,

depending on the complexity of the case.

4. Areas Assessed: The evaluation assesses various aspects of the parents' mental health, including emotional stability, parenting abilities, communication skills, coping mechanisms, and any history of mental health issues or substance abuse. The evaluator may also consider factors such as the parent-child relationship, parenting practices, and the child's attachment to each parent.

5. Child's Best Interests: The evaluation focuses on the best interests of the child and aims to determine which custody arrangement would provide the most stable and nurturing environment for the child's growth and development.

6. Confidentiality and Privacy: The information gathered during the evaluation is typically kept confidential and shared only with the court and relevant parties involved in the case. The evaluator is bound by ethical and legal standards to protect the privacy of those involved.

7. Recommendations: Based on the findings of the evaluation, the mental health professional may provide recommendations to the court regarding child custody and visitation arrangements. The recommendations are intended to guide the court in making a well-informed decision.

It's important to note that mental health and child custody evaluations are complex and can have significant implications for the child and family involved. The process requires sensitivity, thoroughness, and a comprehensive understanding of family dynamics and mental health issues. The ultimate goal is to promote the child's welfare and ensure their well-being in the context of a challenging family situation.

Balancing privacy and intervention for mental health concerns

Balancing privacy and intervention for mental health concerns is a complex and delicate matter. On one hand, privacy is a fundamental right that should be respected and protected. Individuals have the right to keep their personal information, including mental health issues, confidential and private. On the other hand, when mental health concerns arise, intervention and support may be necessary to ensure the well-being and safety of the individual.

Here are some key considerations for balancing privacy and intervention for mental health concerns:

1. Respect for Autonomy: Respecting individuals' autonomy and right to privacy is essential. Mental health issues are highly personal, and individuals may be hesitant to share their struggles due to fear of judgment, stigma, or discrimination. Any intervention or support should be provided in a manner that respects their autonomy and ensures their consent.

2. Mental Health Stigma: The stigma surrounding mental health issues can prevent individuals from seeking help and support. Creating a safe and non-judgmental environment is crucial to encouraging individuals to share their concerns and seek assistance when needed.

3. Informed Consent: Before any intervention or disclosure of information, obtaining informed consent is vital. Individuals should be fully informed about the purpose,

nature, and potential consequences of any intervention, and their consent should be obtained voluntarily and without coercion.

4. Duty to Warn: In some situations, mental health professionals, educators, or caregivers may have a legal or ethical duty to warn or protect others if there is a credible threat of harm to oneself or others. This can be a challenging ethical dilemma, as it involves balancing the individual's right to privacy with the need to prevent potential harm.

5. Confidentiality and Legal Requirements: Mental health professionals, medical providers, and counselors are bound by ethical and legal obligations to maintain confidentiality. However, there are exceptions to confidentiality when mandated by law, such as reporting child abuse, elder abuse, or threats of violence.

6. Supportive Environment: Creating a supportive and caring environment is essential for encouraging individuals to seek help for mental health concerns. This can be achieved through awareness campaigns, education, and reducing stigma associated with mental health.

7. Encouraging Help-Seeking Behavior: Encouraging open discussions about mental health and normalizing help-seeking behavior can make it easier for individuals to reach out for support without feeling judged or stigmatized.

8. Early Intervention: Early intervention is critical in addressing mental health concerns and preventing them from escalating. By promoting early identification and support, privacy concerns can be balanced with timely and appropriate intervention.

In conclusion, balancing privacy and intervention for mental health concerns requires careful consideration of individuals' rights, ethical principles, legal requirements, and the overall goal of ensuring their well-being. Respecting individuals' autonomy, providing a supportive environment, and promoting early intervention are essential steps in achieving this balance. Mental health professionals and caregivers play a crucial role in navigating these complexities and promoting the best interests of those they serve.

Child protection services and legal interventions

Child protection services and legal interventions play a vital role in safeguarding the well-being and safety of children who may be at risk of abuse, neglect, or harm. These services are designed to intervene when there are concerns about a child's welfare and to ensure that appropriate actions are taken to protect the child's best interests. Here are some key aspects of child protection services and legal interventions:

1. Mandated Reporting: In many jurisdictions, certain professionals, such as teachers, healthcare workers, social workers, and law enforcement personnel, are legally obligated to report suspected cases of child abuse or neglect to child protection services. This mandated reporting ensures that potential risks to a child's safety are brought to the attention of the appropriate authorities.

2. Investigation and Assessment: Child protection services typically conduct thorough investigations and assessments when a report of suspected abuse or neglect is received. This may involve interviews with the child, family members, and other relevant individuals, as well as gathering evidence and information from various sources.

3. Risk Assessment: During the investigation, child protection services assess the level of risk to the child's safety and well-being. The risk assessment helps determine the appropriate level of intervention required and the urgency of the situation.

4. Removal and Placement: In severe cases where a child

is at immediate risk of harm, child protection services may remove the child from the home and place them in temporary foster care or with a relative (kinship care). This is done to ensure the child's safety while further assessments and planning take place.

5. Court Involvement: Legal interventions in child protection cases may involve court proceedings. A court may issue orders for the protection of the child, such as temporary custody orders, restraining orders, or orders for supervised visitation.

6. Reunification or Permanency Planning: The goal of child protection services is to promote the best interests of the child. This may involve reunification efforts with the birth family if conditions for safe return are met. In cases where reunification is not possible, child protection services work towards establishing a permanent and stable home for the child, such as adoption or long-term foster care.

7. Support Services: Child protection services also provide support services to families involved in the child protection system. These services may include counseling, parenting classes, substance abuse treatment, or other resources aimed at addressing the underlying issues that led to the child protection intervention.

8. Confidentiality and Privacy: Child protection cases are handled with a high degree of confidentiality to protect the privacy and well-being of the child and the family involved. Information about the case is typically shared on a need-to-know basis among professionals working directly with the family.

Overall, child protection services and legal interventions are essential components of a comprehensive child welfare system. They aim to protect vulnerable children from harm, provide support to families in crisis, and ensure that children have the opportunity to grow up in safe and nurturing environments.

Termination of parental rights and adoption

Termination of parental rights is a legal process by which a court ends the legal relationship between a parent and their child. This can occur for various reasons, such as neglect, abuse, abandonment, or other circumstances where it is deemed that the parent is unable or unwilling to provide a safe and stable environment for the child. Termination of parental rights is a serious and significant decision, as it permanently severs the legal ties between the parent and the child.

Here are some key points to understand about termination of parental rights and adoption:

1. Grounds for Termination: Each jurisdiction has specific laws outlining the grounds for termination of parental rights. These grounds typically include factors such as abuse or neglect, chronic substance abuse, mental illness, abandonment, and failure to provide for the child's basic needs.

2. Legal Process: Termination of parental rights is initiated through a legal petition filed by child protection services or other relevant parties. The court will conduct hearings to evaluate the evidence and determine if grounds for termination exist.

3. Best Interests of the Child: The guiding principle in termination of parental rights cases is the best interests of the child. The court will consider the child's safety, well-being, and need for a stable and permanent home.

4. Permanency Planning: In cases where parental rights are terminated, the focus shifts to permanency planning for the child. The goal is to find a permanent

and stable home for the child, often through adoption.

5. Adoption: Once parental rights are terminated, the child becomes legally eligible for adoption. Prospective adoptive parents may be considered, and the court will assess their suitability to provide a loving and supportive home for the child.

6. Open Adoption: In some cases, an open adoption may be considered, where the birth parents and adoptive parents have ongoing contact and communication with each other and the child.

7. Post-Termination Services: After parental rights are terminated, birth parents may be offered services such as counseling or support to help them cope with the loss and make positive changes in their lives.

8. Legal Representation: Birth parents have the right to legal representation throughout the termination process. If they cannot afford an attorney, one may be appointed for them.

Termination of parental rights is a complex and emotionally charged process that can have profound and lasting effects on the lives of everyone involved. It is crucial to ensure that all decisions are made in the best interests of the child and that the child's well-being and safety remain the top priorities throughout the legal proceedings. Adoption, when appropriate, provides the opportunity for a child to be embraced by a loving and supportive family, offering them the chance to thrive and grow in a stable and nurturing environment.

Foster care and kinship care arrangements

Foster care and kinship care arrangements are two important options for providing temporary or permanent care for children who are unable to live with their birth parents due to various reasons. Both types of care involve placing a child in the custody of a caregiver other than their birth parents, but they differ in certain aspects.

1. Foster Care:
    - Foster care is a system in which children are placed in the temporary care of licensed foster parents or foster families.
    - It is often used when children cannot live with their birth parents due to issues like neglect, abuse, or parental incapacity.
    - Foster care is designed to provide a safe and supportive environment for children while their birth parents work to resolve the issues that led to the separation.
    - Foster parents receive training and support to meet the physical, emotional, and developmental needs of the children in their care.
    - The goal of foster care is typically reunification with the birth parents, but if that is not possible, other permanency options such as adoption may be pursued.

2. Kinship Care:
    - Kinship care refers to the placement of a child with a relative, such as a grandparent, aunt,

uncle, or adult sibling, when the child cannot live with their birth parents.

- Kinship care is often preferred when possible, as it allows children to stay within their extended family network, maintaining important connections and cultural ties.
- Kinship caregivers may or may not be licensed as foster parents, depending on the jurisdiction and the specific circumstances of the placement.
- Like foster parents, kinship caregivers are responsible for meeting the child's needs and providing a stable and loving environment.

Differences and Similarities:

- Both foster care and kinship care aim to provide children with safe and stable living arrangements when they cannot live with their birth parents.
- Foster care is often managed by child welfare agencies, while kinship care may involve the involvement of family courts.
- Foster care is typically regulated by specific licensing requirements, whereas kinship care may have more flexible arrangements, depending on local laws and policies.
- Both types of care can be temporary or permanent, depending on the specific circumstances and decisions made by the court or child welfare authorities.

It is essential for both foster care and kinship care arrangements to prioritize the best interests of the child, providing them with a supportive and nurturing environment that fosters their growth and well-being. Regardless of the type of care, caregivers play a critical role in helping children heal from any past trauma and build healthy and positive relationships. The ultimate goal is to ensure that children in need of care are placed in safe and loving homes where they can thrive and reach their full potential.

The role of family law in ensuring child well-being

Family law plays a vital role in ensuring child well-being by establishing legal frameworks that protect children's rights, safety, and overall welfare. It addresses various aspects of children's lives, including custody, visitation, child support, and child protection. Here are some key ways family law promotes child well-being:

1. Custody and Visitation: Family law governs child custody arrangements, ensuring that decisions are made in the best interests of the child. It considers factors such as the child's safety, emotional and physical needs, stability, and the ability of each parent or caregiver to provide a suitable environment. Custody orders aim to maintain meaningful relationships with both parents whenever possible, supporting the child's emotional well-being through consistent contact with both parents.

2. Child Support: Family law establishes guidelines for determining child support payments to ensure that both parents financially contribute to the child's upbringing. Adequate child support helps provide for the child's basic needs, including food, clothing, shelter, education, and healthcare.

3. Protection from Abuse and Neglect: Family law includes provisions for child protection and intervention when a child is subjected to abuse or neglect. This may involve removing the child from an unsafe environment and

placing them in foster care or with relatives, with the goal of ensuring their immediate safety and well-being.

4. Adoption and Foster Care: Family law governs the legal process of adoption, ensuring that children are placed with suitable and loving families. It also regulates the licensing and oversight of foster care providers to ensure that children in temporary care receive proper support and protection.

5. Paternity Determination: Family law addresses issues related to paternity, establishing legal fatherhood and parental rights, which is essential for determining custody, visitation, and child support arrangements.

6. Mediation and Dispute Resolution: Family law encourages mediation and alternative dispute resolution methods to resolve conflicts and custody disputes amicably, promoting a less adversarial environment that can benefit the child's emotional well-being.

7. Emphasis on Child's Best Interests: Throughout the legal process, family law places the child's best interests as the primary consideration. Courts and authorities strive to make decisions that safeguard the child's physical, emotional, and developmental needs.

8. Legal Representation: Family law ensures that children have access to legal representation or guardians ad litem in cases where their rights or interests are at stake, helping to protect their rights and ensure their voices are heard.

By providing legal structures that prioritize children's well-being, family law seeks to create stable and nurturing environments where children can grow, thrive, and develop into healthy and happy individuals. It recognizes the significant impact that family dynamics can have on a child's life and aims to ensure that children's needs are met and their rights protected throughout any legal proceedings related to their care and upbringing.

Consent and treatment decisions for minors

Consent and treatment decisions for minors are complex legal and ethical issues that involve balancing the rights of parents or legal guardians with the best interests of the child. The laws regarding consent for medical treatment of minors vary across jurisdictions, but some common principles and considerations include:

1. Age of Consent: In many countries, the age at which a minor can provide their own consent for medical treatment varies. Typically, teenagers who have reached a certain age, often around 16 or 18, may have the right to make their own medical decisions without parental consent.

2. Emancipated Minors: Some minors are considered "emancipated" and have the legal capacity to consent to medical treatment independently of their parents. Emancipation can occur through marriage, military service, or a court order.

3. Mature Minor Doctrine: In some jurisdictions, minors who demonstrate sufficient maturity and understanding of the consequences of medical treatment may be allowed to consent to specific medical procedures, even if they are not yet of the age of majority.

4. Parental Consent: For younger minors who do not have the legal capacity to consent, parental or legal guardian consent is usually required for medical treatment. Parents or guardians are responsible for making decisions in the best interests of their child's health and well-being.

5. Emergencies: In emergency situations where immediate medical treatment is required to save a minor's life or prevent serious harm, medical professionals may provide treatment without obtaining consent from parents or guardians.

6. Medical Consent Laws: Some jurisdictions have specific laws that outline the circumstances under which minors can consent to certain medical treatments, such as reproductive health services, mental health treatment, and substance abuse treatment.

7. Court Involvement: In cases of disagreement between parents or guardians regarding medical treatment for a minor, a court may need to intervene to determine what is in the child's best interests.

8. Ethical Considerations: Healthcare providers must consider the ethical principles of beneficence, non-maleficence, autonomy, and justice when making decisions about medical treatment for minors.

9. Confidentiality: Healthcare providers must balance a minor's right to confidentiality with their obligation to inform parents or guardians about the minor's medical condition and treatment plan.

It is important for healthcare providers, parents, and legal guardians to be aware of the specific laws and guidelines in their jurisdiction regarding consent and treatment decisions for minors. Open communication between healthcare providers, parents, and minors is essential to ensure that the child's health needs are met while respecting their rights and autonomy to the greatest extent possible within the legal framework.

Emancipated minors and medical autonomy

Emancipated minors are individuals who have been granted legal independence from their parents or guardians before reaching the age of majority. This legal status allows them to have certain rights and responsibilities typically reserved for adults. One significant aspect of emancipation is the grant of medical autonomy, which means that an emancipated minor has the right to make their own medical decisions without requiring parental or guardian consent.

The process of emancipation varies depending on the jurisdiction, but it generally involves the minor demonstrating to the court that they are financially self-sufficient, capable of managing their affairs, and have a compelling reason for seeking emancipation. Common reasons for seeking emancipation include situations of abuse or neglect, pursuing educational or career opportunities, or getting married at a young age.

Once a minor is emancipated, they can legally consent to medical treatment, including surgical procedures, mental health treatment, and reproductive health services, without involving their parents or legal guardians. Emancipated minors are treated as adults in terms of their medical decision-making, and healthcare providers must respect their autonomy.

However, it is important to note that not all medical decisions are left solely to the minor's discretion. Healthcare providers must still ensure that the minor has the capacity to understand the nature and consequences of the medical treatment and can provide informed consent. If a healthcare provider believes that the minor lacks the capacity to make a particular medical decision, they may need to seek court involvement or consider other legal options to protect the minor's best interests.

Emancipation and medical autonomy are crucial in situations where minors may have legitimate reasons for seeking independence from their parents or guardians. These legal protections ensure that emancipated minors have control over their healthcare decisions and are not subject to potential barriers or coercion from others. However, healthcare providers must approach each case individually and carefully assess the minor's capacity to make informed medical decisions to uphold the principles of beneficence, non-maleficence, autonomy, and justice.

Parental rights and medical decision-making conflicts

Parental rights and medical decision-making conflicts can arise in various situations where parents or legal guardians have differing views on the medical treatment of their child. These conflicts can be emotionally charged and complex, involving legal, ethical, and moral considerations. Here are some common scenarios and factors that can lead to conflicts:

1. Medical Treatment Options: Parents may disagree on the appropriate medical treatment for their child. This can involve decisions about surgery, medications, therapies, or alternative treatments.
2. Religious or Cultural Beliefs: Some parents may hold strong religious or cultural beliefs that influence their views on medical treatments. These beliefs may conflict with medical recommendations or standard practices.
3. End-of-Life Decisions: In cases of severe illness or terminal conditions, parents may disagree on whether to continue life-sustaining treatments, opt for palliative care, or pursue other approaches.
4. Mental Health Treatment: Conflicts can arise when one parent supports a specific mental health treatment for the child, while the other prefers an alternative approach or denies the need for treatment altogether.
5. Vaccination: Vaccination decisions can be contentious for some parents, leading to conflicts over whether to vaccinate the child or not.
6. Custody Arrangements: In cases of divorced or

separated parents, conflicts may arise if one parent has primary custody and makes medical decisions without consulting the other parent.

7. Second Opinions: Parents may seek second opinions from different healthcare providers, leading to conflicting treatment recommendations.

When parental rights and medical decision-making conflicts occur, it is essential to prioritize the best interests of the child. In most jurisdictions, the legal standard used to resolve these conflicts is the "best interests of the child." Courts may step in to make decisions if parents cannot reach an agreement.

To address conflicts and ensure that the child's well-being remains the primary focus, healthcare providers may:

- Communicate openly and transparently with both parents, providing them with all relevant information to make informed decisions.
- Encourage parents to engage in dialogue with each other and with the healthcare team to reach a consensus whenever possible.
- Consider seeking a court-appointed guardian ad litem or mediator to represent the child's interests and provide impartial guidance.
- Follow applicable legal procedures and guidelines in cases where a court order is required to proceed with medical treatment.
- Document all communication and decisions carefully to establish a clear record of the decision-making process.

Ultimately, resolving conflicts in medical decision-making requires collaboration, empathy, and a commitment to the well-being of the child. Healthcare providers play a crucial role in facilitating communication and helping parents navigate these challenging situations.

Legal aspects of medical treatment for minors

The legal aspects of medical treatment for minors can be complex and vary depending on the jurisdiction and specific circumstances. In general, minors are not considered legally competent to make medical decisions for themselves, and their parents or legal guardians typically have the authority to make medical decisions on their behalf. However, there are several important legal considerations:

1. Informed Consent: In most cases, parents or legal guardians must provide informed consent for medical treatment on behalf of their minor child. Informed consent means that the parents are fully informed about the nature of the treatment, its potential risks and benefits, and any alternative options before making a decision.

2. Mature Minors: In some jurisdictions, certain minors who are considered "mature minors" may have the legal capacity to consent to their own medical treatment. The definition of a mature minor and the extent of their decision-making capacity may vary by jurisdiction.

3. Emancipated Minors: In some cases, minors who have been emancipated through court order or legal means may have the legal right to consent to medical treatment on their own behalf, without requiring parental consent.

4. Emergency Situations: In emergency situations where immediate medical treatment is required to save a minor's life or prevent serious harm, medical providers may provide treatment without obtaining formal

consent if it is not feasible to obtain consent from the parents.

5. Medical Decision-Making Conflicts: As mentioned earlier, conflicts may arise between parents or legal guardians regarding medical treatment decisions for a minor. In such cases, courts may become involved to determine the best course of action in the child's best interests.

6. Medical Records and Privacy: Minors' medical records are generally considered private and protected by laws such as the Health Insurance Portability and Accountability Act (HIPAA) in the United States. Parents or legal guardians usually have access to their child's medical records, but there may be exceptions for sensitive information related to certain conditions.

7. Mental Health Treatment: In cases involving mental health treatment, specific laws and regulations may apply, especially if the minor requires psychiatric hospitalization or treatment for a mental health crisis.

It is crucial for healthcare providers to be aware of the specific laws and regulations governing medical treatment for minors in their jurisdiction and to ensure compliance with these legal requirements. In cases of uncertainty or conflicts, seeking legal counsel or involving an ethics committee may be necessary to navigate the complexities of medical decision-making for minors. The overarching goal is to ensure that the minor's health and well-being are protected while respecting their rights and the rights of their parents or legal guardians.

Physician-assisted dying and right to die

Physician-assisted dying, also known as medical aid in dying or the right to die, refers to the practice where a terminally ill or suffering patient seeks medical assistance to hasten their death. This controversial topic raises complex ethical, legal, and moral questions. The debate revolves around individual autonomy, the right to self-determination, and the duty of physicians to alleviate suffering.

The arguments in favor of physician-assisted dying often emphasize personal autonomy and the right of individuals to make decisions about their own lives, including how they die. Advocates argue that terminally ill patients who are experiencing unbearable suffering should have the option to end their lives with medical assistance, allowing them to die with dignity and on their own terms.

On the other side, opponents of physician-assisted dying are concerned about potential abuses, the slippery slope towards euthanasia, and the ethical implications for medical professionals. Some argue that allowing physicians to participate in assisted dying goes against the fundamental principles of medicine, which include preserving life and alleviating suffering. They believe that the focus should be on improving palliative care and providing support for patients during their end-of-life journey.

The legality of physician-assisted dying varies around the world. Some countries and states have enacted laws that allow for medically assisted dying under specific conditions, while others prohibit it entirely. In regions where it is legal, there are typically strict eligibility criteria and procedural safeguards in place to ensure that the process is not abused and that patients' decisions are well-informed and voluntary.

The issue of physician-assisted dying continues to be a deeply contentious and emotional topic that elicits strong reactions from people with different beliefs and values. As society grapples with the complexities of end-of-life care and the ethical implications of individual choice, the conversation surrounding physician-assisted dying remains an ongoing and evolving dialogue.

Advance healthcare directives and living wills

Advance healthcare directives and living wills are legal documents that allow individuals to express their preferences for medical treatment in the event that they become unable to make decisions for themselves due to illness or incapacitation. These documents provide a way for individuals to retain control over their medical care and ensure that their wishes are respected, even if they are unable to communicate them directly.

A living will is a written document that outlines a person's preferences for medical treatment and end-of-life care. It typically includes instructions about the use of life-sustaining treatments, such as mechanical ventilation, tube feeding, and resuscitation. By specifying their wishes in advance, individuals can guide their healthcare providers and loved ones in making decisions on their behalf if they become unable to express their preferences.

An advance healthcare directive, also known as a medical power of attorney or healthcare proxy, is a legal document that designates a trusted person, known as a healthcare agent or proxy, to make medical decisions on behalf of the individual if they are unable to do so. The appointed proxy is authorized to act as the individual's advocate, ensuring that their wishes are honored and medical decisions are made in their best interest.

These documents are essential tools for ensuring that individuals maintain control over their healthcare decisions, even when they are unable to communicate their preferences. They are particularly valuable in situations where medical treatment options are uncertain, and important decisions need to be made quickly.

The specific requirements and regulations for advance healthcare directives and living wills may vary by jurisdiction. It is important for individuals to understand the legal requirements in their region and to work with an attorney or healthcare professional to draft these documents properly.

By creating advance healthcare directives and living wills, individuals can gain peace of mind knowing that their medical care will align with their values and beliefs, and their loved ones will be informed about their healthcare wishes in difficult times. These documents empower individuals to have a voice in their medical care, even when they are unable to speak for themselves.

Hospice and palliative care legal considerations

Hospice and palliative care are specialized medical services that focus on providing comfort and support to individuals facing serious illnesses, particularly those in the final stages of life. These forms of care prioritize pain management, symptom relief, emotional support, and improving the overall quality of life for patients.

From a legal perspective, there are several important considerations related to hospice and palliative care:

1. Consent and Decision-Making: Patients must provide informed consent for hospice and palliative care services. This means they should be fully informed about the nature of the care, its benefits, and potential risks before agreeing to receive it. If a patient is unable to make decisions, their legally designated healthcare proxy or surrogate decision-maker may give consent on their behalf, following any advance directives or living wills the patient may have executed.

2. Medical Orders: Hospice and palliative care require specific medical orders from a qualified healthcare provider. These orders outline the type and extent of care to be provided, including medications, pain management, and any life-sustaining treatments to be withheld or withdrawn.

3. Legal Documentation: It is essential to have clear legal documentation in place, such as advance healthcare

directives and living wills, to ensure that the patient's end-of-life wishes are respected and followed by healthcare providers.

4. Confidentiality and Privacy: Patient confidentiality and privacy must be rigorously maintained in hospice and palliative care settings to protect sensitive medical information and honor the patient's dignity.

5. Guardianship: In cases where a patient lacks the capacity to make healthcare decisions and has not designated a healthcare proxy, a court-appointed guardian may be involved in making decisions about hospice and palliative care.

6. Family Consent: Hospice and palliative care often involve family members or close friends who play an important role in supporting the patient. It is crucial to obtain the consent of both the patient and their family for the care plan.

7. Insurance and Payment: Understanding insurance coverage and payment options for hospice and palliative care is important. Many healthcare plans, including Medicare and Medicaid, offer coverage for these services.

8. Compliance with Regulations: Hospice and palliative care providers must comply with local, state, and federal regulations governing their services to ensure high-quality care and patient safety.

It is essential for patients and their families to be well-informed about their rights and options related to hospice and palliative care. Engaging in open and honest communication with healthcare providers and seeking legal counsel when necessary can help ensure that patients receive the appropriate care that aligns with their values and preferences during challenging times.

The role of family law in end-of-life decisions

Family law plays a significant role in end-of-life decisions, particularly when it comes to healthcare choices and making decisions for individuals who are unable to do so themselves. In the context of end-of-life care, family law addresses several critical aspects:

1. Healthcare Proxy and Surrogate Decision-Making: Family law allows individuals to designate a healthcare proxy or surrogate decision-maker, often through a durable power of attorney for healthcare. This legal document empowers a trusted person, typically a family member, to make medical decisions on behalf of the individual if they become incapacitated or are unable to communicate their preferences.

2. Living Wills and Advance Directives: These legal documents allow individuals to express their end-of-life wishes, such as preferences for life-sustaining treatments, organ donation, and other medical interventions. Family law ensures that these directives are legally binding and followed by healthcare providers and family members.

3. Guardianship: In situations where a person lacks the capacity to make healthcare decisions and has not appointed a healthcare proxy or surrogate decision-maker, family law allows for the appointment of a legal guardian. The guardian is authorized to make decisions related to the individual's healthcare, including end-of-life choices.

4. Family Disputes: End-of-life decisions can sometimes

lead to disagreements among family members regarding the best course of action for the patient. Family law can help resolve these disputes through mediation or court intervention to ensure that decisions are made in the patient's best interest.

5. Minors and End-of-Life Care: Family law addresses end-of-life decisions for minors, including the roles and rights of parents or legal guardians in making healthcare choices for their children. In some cases, court approval may be required for certain medical treatments or end-of-life decisions involving minors.

6. Capacity Assessment: Family law may be involved in determining a person's capacity to make healthcare decisions. Courts may be called upon to assess an individual's mental and cognitive abilities when questions arise about their ability to understand and express their end-of-life preferences.

7. Termination of Life Support: In cases where an individual is on life support, family law may be invoked to decide whether to continue or terminate life-sustaining treatment based on the patient's previously expressed wishes or the consensus of family members.

8. Legal Protections for Healthcare Providers: Family law also offers legal protections for healthcare providers who comply with patients' advance directives and end-of-life decisions, shielding them from potential liability in situations where care aligns with the patient's expressed wishes.

The role of family law in end-of-life decisions is vital in ensuring that patients' rights are respected, their wishes are honored, and their best interests are upheld during challenging times. Having a clear understanding of family law provisions and engaging in open communication with family members and healthcare providers can facilitate a more compassionate and supportive end-of-life journey for all involved.

Legal implications of genetic testing and screening

Genetic testing and screening have significant legal implications, raising important ethical, privacy, and discrimination concerns. Some of the key legal aspects associated with genetic testing and screening include:

1. Informed Consent: Individuals must provide informed consent before undergoing genetic testing or screening. This consent ensures that they understand the purpose, potential risks, and benefits of the tests, as well as the possible implications of the results.

2. Genetic Discrimination: Concerns about genetic discrimination have led to the passage of laws to protect individuals from discrimination based on genetic information. In many jurisdictions, laws prohibit employers and health insurers from using genetic information to make decisions about employment, insurance coverage, or premiums.

3. Privacy and Confidentiality: Genetic information is highly sensitive and personal. Legal frameworks are in place to safeguard the privacy and confidentiality of genetic data, ensuring that it is only shared with authorized individuals or entities.

4. Genetic Information Nondiscrimination Act (GINA): In the United States, GINA is a federal law that prohibits health insurers and employers from discriminating against individuals based on their genetic information.

5. Patents and Intellectual Property: The ownership and

patenting of genes and genetic information have sparked legal debates and challenges. Some countries have strict regulations regarding the patenting of genetic material to ensure broad access to genetic testing and research.

6. Prenatal Testing and Reproductive Rights: Legal issues arise in the context of prenatal genetic testing, such as noninvasive prenatal testing (NIPT). Questions may arise about the right to access such testing, the use of the results to inform reproductive choices, and the duty to disclose certain genetic conditions.

7. Family Law and Genetic Testing: Genetic testing can have implications for family relationships, such as paternity disputes or determining genetic predispositions to specific conditions that could impact family planning.

8. Forensic DNA Databases: The use of DNA databases for forensic purposes raises concerns about privacy, accuracy, and potential misuse of genetic information.

9. Regulation of Genetic Testing Laboratories: Laws and regulations govern the operation of genetic testing laboratories to ensure accuracy, quality control, and patient safety.

10. Pharmacogenomics: The use of genetic information to tailor medication and treatment plans raises issues related to medical liability, informed consent, and the interpretation of genetic data.

11. Research and Informed Consent: Researchers collecting and using genetic data must adhere to strict ethical guidelines, obtaining informed consent from participants and protecting their privacy.

As genetic testing and screening technologies continue to advance, legal frameworks will need to adapt to address new challenges and protect the rights of individuals while facilitating the responsible and beneficial use of genetic information for medical research and healthcare.

Preimplantation genetic diagnosis and legalities

Preimplantation Genetic Diagnosis (PGD) is a medical procedure used during in vitro fertilization (IVF) to screen embryos for genetic abnormalities before they are implanted in the uterus. It involves the removal of one or more cells from an embryo to analyze its genetic makeup.

The legalities surrounding PGD vary from country to country and are subject to evolving regulations and ethical considerations. Some key legal aspects of PGD include:

1. Permissible Conditions: Different jurisdictions have guidelines on which genetic conditions can be screened using PGD. Some countries allow PGD for serious genetic disorders, while others may extend it to include conditions with a lower impact on health.
2. Ethical Considerations: PGD raises ethical questions about the selection of embryos based on genetic traits. Some concerns revolve around issues of eugenics, disability rights, and the potential for "designer babies."
3. Informed Consent: Patients undergoing IVF with PGD must provide informed consent, understanding the purpose and potential implications of the procedure.
4. Parental Decision-making: Decisions regarding PGD, including which embryos to implant, are typically made by the parents. Legal and ethical discussions center around the right of parents to make these decisions and the duty of healthcare providers to provide accurate

information.

5. Embryo Disposition: Laws may govern the disposition of embryos not chosen for implantation, including options for donation, storage, or destruction.

6. Privacy and Confidentiality: Genetic information obtained through PGD is highly sensitive and must be protected under existing privacy and confidentiality laws.

7. Regulation of IVF Clinics: Countries have regulations to oversee IVF clinics offering PGD to ensure the safety and ethical conduct of the procedure.

8. Gender Selection: Some countries have restrictions on gender selection for non-medical reasons, and the use of PGD for gender selection may be subject to specific laws.

9. Religious and Cultural Perspectives: In some cultures and religions, there may be differing views on the acceptability of PGD and its applications.

10. International Differences: Laws and regulations surrounding PGD can differ significantly between countries, leading to issues when patients from one country seek PGD treatment abroad.

As the field of reproductive technologies continues to advance, policymakers and lawmakers will face ongoing challenges in striking a balance between promoting scientific progress, respecting individual autonomy, and upholding ethical principles. Legal frameworks related to PGD will need to adapt to address new ethical and technological considerations while ensuring the well-being and rights of all involved parties.

Genetic information and family law disputes

Genetic information can play a significant role in family law disputes, especially in cases involving parentage, child custody, and support. Here are some ways genetic information may impact family law matters:

1. Paternity and Parentage: Genetic testing, such as DNA testing, can be used to determine the biological relationship between a parent and a child. In cases where paternity is in question or disputed, a court may order genetic testing to establish or disprove parentage.

2. Child Custody and Visitation: In child custody disputes, genetic information can be relevant in determining a biological connection between a parent and a child. Courts may consider genetic testing results in making custody and visitation decisions.

3. Child Support: The determination of child support may be affected by genetic information. If paternity is established through genetic testing, the court may order child support from the biological parent.

4. Inheritance and Estate Planning: Genetic information may be relevant in cases involving inheritance and estate planning. It can help establish relationships between potential heirs and beneficiaries.

5. Surrogacy and Assisted Reproduction: In cases involving surrogacy or assisted reproduction, genetic information may be used to establish parentage and legal rights of intended parents.

6. Medical History and Health Issues: Genetic information can provide valuable insights into potential health risks

and conditions that may impact child custody and parental responsibilities.

7. Adoption: In adoption cases, genetic information about the child's birth parents may be relevant to consider when determining the best interests of the child.

8. Confidentiality and Privacy: Legal issues related to the privacy and confidentiality of genetic information may arise in family law cases. Courts and legal professionals must handle genetic data with sensitivity and in accordance with applicable laws.

It is important to note that the use of genetic information in family law cases must be done in accordance with relevant laws and regulations. The admissibility and handling of genetic evidence may vary by jurisdiction, and legal professionals should ensure that the collection and use of genetic information comply with ethical and legal standards.

Overall, genetic information can be a valuable tool in family law disputes, providing clarity on parentage and biological relationships. However, it is crucial to approach such information with caution and sensitivity, considering the potential impact on individuals and families involved in the legal proceedings.

Ethical dilemmas in genetic technologies

Genetic technologies have advanced rapidly in recent years, leading to numerous ethical dilemmas that society must grapple with. Some of the key ethical challenges associated with genetic technologies include:

1. Privacy and Confidentiality: Genetic information is highly personal and sensitive. Ensuring the privacy and confidentiality of individuals' genetic data is crucial to prevent discrimination and stigmatization based on genetic traits or predispositions.

2. Informed Consent: Obtaining informed consent from individuals before conducting genetic testing or using their genetic data is essential. People must be fully aware of the potential risks, benefits, and implications of genetic testing and research.

3. Genetic Discrimination: Concerns exist about the potential for genetic discrimination in areas such as employment, insurance, and education. Genetic information could be used to deny individuals access to opportunities or resources.

4. Access and Equity: Ensuring equitable access to genetic technologies and the benefits they offer is a challenge. Socioeconomic disparities could exacerbate existing inequalities in healthcare and genetic testing availability.

5. Reproductive Decision-making: Genetic technologies like preimplantation genetic diagnosis (PGD) raise ethical questions about selecting embryos based on specific genetic traits, potentially leading to eugenics

concerns.

6. Genetic Editing: The development of gene editing technologies, such as CRISPR-Cas9, raises ethical concerns about the potential for "designer babies" and the long-term consequences of altering the human germline.

7. Ownership of Genetic Data: Determining who owns and controls an individual's genetic data is an ethical challenge, especially when genetic information is shared for research or commercial purposes.

8. Genetic Testing in Minors: The use of genetic testing in minors can be ethically complex, especially when it involves adult-onset conditions that may not manifest until later in life.

9. Genetic Testing for Non-Medical Purposes: The use of genetic testing for non-medical purposes, such as ancestry testing or identifying unrelated family members, raises ethical questions about privacy and consent.

10. Cross-Border Genetic Research: Ethical challenges arise when conducting genetic research across borders, as different countries may have varying regulations and ethical standards.

11. Genetic Testing in Decision-making: The implications of genetic testing in making life-altering decisions, such as reproductive choices or preventive surgeries, require careful consideration of ethical principles.

Addressing these ethical dilemmas requires an interdisciplinary approach involving geneticists, healthcare professionals, ethicists, policymakers, and the broader public. Balancing individual autonomy, privacy, and societal well-being is essential to ensure that genetic technologies are used responsibly and ethically. Continued dialogue and ongoing ethical assessments are necessary as genetic technologies continue to evolve and impact various aspects of society.

Family law during pandemics and health crises

Family law during pandemics and health crises becomes especially crucial as these circumstances can significantly impact family dynamics and legal rights. Some of the key issues and considerations in family law during pandemics and health crises include:

1. Child Custody and Visitation: Health crises may disrupt regular custody arrangements, leading to challenges in visitation and parenting time. Courts and parents need to find creative and flexible solutions to ensure the well-being of children while respecting health guidelines and restrictions.

2. Child Support: Economic hardships during pandemics can affect the ability of parents to meet their child support obligations. Family courts may need to address modifications in support orders based on changes in financial circumstances.

3. Domestic Violence: During periods of stress and isolation, incidents of domestic violence may increase. Family law courts need to remain accessible to address protection orders and provide support and resources to victims.

4. Divorce and Separation: The strains of a health crisis can place additional stress on marriages and relationships, leading to an increase in divorce and separation rates. Legal processes related to divorce, property division, and alimony may be impacted.

5. Adoption and Foster Care: Health crises may affect adoption and foster care processes, leading to delays and adjustments in court proceedings.
6. Medical Decision-making: Family law may come into play when determining who has the legal authority to make medical decisions for family members who are incapacitated or unable to communicate their preferences.
7. Guardianship and Conservatorship: Health crises may result in situations where individuals require guardians or conservators to make decisions on their behalf due to illness or incapacity.
8. Estate Planning: Health crises can serve as a reminder of the importance of estate planning, including wills, trusts, and advance healthcare directives, to ensure that individuals' wishes are legally protected.
9. Virtual Court Proceedings: Family courts may need to adapt to virtual hearings and proceedings to ensure access to justice while maintaining health and safety measures.
10. Access to Legal Services: Economic hardships during a health crisis may limit access to legal services for some individuals. Ensuring affordable and accessible legal representation becomes critical.
11. Parental Rights and Medical Decisions: Health crises can raise questions about parental rights and the ability to make medical decisions for children, especially if one parent disagrees with certain medical treatments.

Family law practitioners, judges, policymakers, and community organizations must work together to address these unique challenges during pandemics and health crises. Ensuring that legal systems remain responsive, empathetic, and adaptive to changing circumstances is vital to protect the rights and well-being of families during these challenging times.

Parental rights and health emergency decisions

Parental rights and health emergency decisions are complex legal issues that arise when a child's health and well-being are at stake during a crisis or emergency. During such situations, quick and well-informed decisions need to be made to protect the child's health while also respecting the rights and responsibilities of the parents.

Here are some key points to consider regarding parental rights and health emergency decisions:

1. Best Interest of the Child: The paramount consideration in any health emergency decision involving a child is the best interest of the child. Courts and authorities prioritize the child's safety, health, and welfare when making decisions.

2. Legal Custody and Decision-Making Authority: The custodial and decision-making rights of parents are typically outlined in child custody orders or agreements. In the case of joint custody, both parents may have equal say in medical decisions. In sole custody arrangements, the custodial parent usually has the authority to make medical decisions.

3. Consent for Medical Treatment: In non-emergency situations, both parents usually need to provide consent for major medical treatment for their child. However, during a health emergency, when immediate action is required, one parent may be allowed to provide consent if the other parent is unavailable or cannot be reached in a timely manner.

4. Disagreements between Parents: If parents disagree on a medical treatment during a health emergency, the court may need to intervene and make a determination based on the child's best interest and expert medical advice.

5. Temporary Custody Orders: In some cases, health emergencies may lead to temporary changes in custody orders if a child's primary residence is in an affected area or if one parent is unavailable due to quarantine or other reasons.

6. Parental Visitation and Contact: Health emergencies may affect visitation schedules and parental contact, especially if one parent or a member of their household is exposed to the virus.

7. Medical Privacy and Confidentiality: Medical information about a child is generally confidential. However, during health emergencies, health care providers may need to share essential medical information with both parents to ensure proper care.

8. Advance Healthcare Directives: Parents may consider having advance healthcare directives in place for their child, specifying their wishes for medical treatment and decision-making in the event of a health emergency.

9. Court Orders and State Laws: Different states have varying laws regarding parental rights and emergency decisions. Court orders and custody agreements should be reviewed to understand the legal framework in place.

In any health emergency involving a child, clear communication, cooperation, and access to professional legal advice are essential to navigate the complexities of parental rights and health decisions. If parents are unable to reach an agreement, they may need to seek legal guidance or involve the court to make informed decisions that prioritize the child's welfare.

Medical treatment and consent during emergencies

Medical treatment and consent during emergencies is a critical aspect of healthcare that aims to provide timely and necessary care to individuals in life-threatening situations while respecting their rights and autonomy. Emergency medical treatment often requires quick decisions and immediate action to save lives, and this can pose challenges in obtaining traditional informed consent.

Here are some key points related to medical treatment and consent during emergencies:

1. Implied Consent: In emergencies where a patient is unable to provide consent due to their condition (e.g., unconsciousness or severe injury), medical professionals often rely on the principle of "implied consent." Implied consent assumes that a reasonable person, if able to provide consent, would agree to receive life-saving medical treatment.

2. Good Samaritan Laws: Good Samaritan laws protect individuals who provide emergency medical care in good faith from liability, even if they do not have explicit consent. These laws encourage bystanders and first responders to act promptly in emergency situations.

3. Next of Kin or Emergency Contacts: In cases where a patient is unable to provide consent, medical professionals may attempt to contact the patient's next of kin or emergency contacts to obtain consent or gather

relevant medical information.

4. Exigent Circumstances: In some situations, the urgency of the emergency may not allow for explicit consent. Medical professionals must use their judgment and training to make decisions that are in the best interest of the patient.

5. Life-Threatening Situations: Emergency medical treatment is often provided to stabilize a patient's condition and prevent immediate harm. Once the patient is stable, efforts are made to seek explicit consent for further treatment.

6. Minor Patients: In the case of minors, consent is usually sought from parents or legal guardians. However, if immediate treatment is required and parents cannot be reached, medical professionals may proceed with treatment under the principle of implied consent.

7. Advance Directives: Patients who have prepared advance healthcare directives, living wills, or durable power of attorney for healthcare can provide guidance on their treatment preferences during emergencies.

8. Incapacitated Adults: For adults who are incapacitated and do not have a designated healthcare proxy or advance directive, medical professionals may seek consent from family members or consult a medical ethics committee.

9. Crisis Standards of Care: During large-scale emergencies or disasters, healthcare facilities may implement crisis standards of care that prioritize limited resources to save the greatest number of lives.

It is essential for healthcare providers to prioritize the safety and well-being of patients during emergencies while adhering to ethical principles and legal regulations. Communication and collaboration with patients, families, and legal representatives play a crucial role in ensuring that appropriate and informed decisions are made in the context of emergency medical treatment.

Legal aspects of quarantine and isolation measures

Quarantine and isolation measures play a significant role in controlling the spread of infectious diseases and protecting public health during outbreaks or pandemics. These measures may be implemented by governments and health authorities to prevent the transmission of contagious diseases to others. While quarantine and isolation are critical tools in public health, they also raise legal and ethical considerations to safeguard individuals' rights and well-being. Here are some key legal aspects of quarantine and isolation measures:

1. Public Health Laws: Many countries have specific public health laws that grant authorities the power to implement quarantine and isolation measures to control the spread of infectious diseases. These laws often define the scope and duration of quarantine and isolation, the conditions for their implementation, and the penalties for non-compliance.

2. Voluntary vs. Compulsory Measures: In some cases, individuals may be asked to voluntarily quarantine or isolate themselves if they have been exposed to a contagious disease or are at risk of spreading it. However, authorities may impose compulsory measures when voluntary compliance is not sufficient to control the disease's spread.

3. Due Process: When enforcing quarantine or isolation, individuals have the right to due process, which

includes being informed of the reasons for their quarantine, having access to legal representation, and the ability to challenge the measures in a court of law if necessary.

4. Duration of Quarantine and Isolation: The length of quarantine and isolation periods may vary depending on the disease's incubation period and the individual's risk of transmission. Authorities must ensure that these periods are based on scientific evidence and regularly reviewed to protect public health without unnecessarily infringing on individual rights.

5. Accommodations for Vulnerable Populations: Special considerations are made for vulnerable populations, such as elderly individuals, pregnant women, and individuals with disabilities, to ensure that their rights are protected during quarantine and isolation.

6. Compensation and Support: In some cases, individuals who are placed under quarantine or isolation may experience financial hardship due to missed work or other economic impacts. Legal frameworks may provide compensation and support for affected individuals to alleviate the burden.

7. Public Information and Communication: Transparency and clear communication with the public are essential during quarantine and isolation measures. Authorities should provide timely and accurate information about the reasons for the measures, their expected duration, and the steps individuals can take to protect themselves and others.

8. Enforcement and Penalties: Legal frameworks may define enforcement mechanisms and penalties for non-compliance with quarantine and isolation orders. These penalties are intended to deter non-compliance and protect public health but should be proportional and fair.

9. Ethical Considerations: Ethical principles, such as proportionality, beneficence, and respect for autonomy, should guide the implementation of quarantine and isolation measures to strike a balance between protecting public health and respecting individual rights and dignity.

10. International Law: International health regulations and treaties may also impact the implementation of quarantine and isolation measures, especially when diseases cross national borders.

It is crucial for quarantine and isolation measures to be carried out with sensitivity to individual rights and in accordance with legal and ethical principles to effectively combat infectious diseases while upholding human rights and human dignity.

Balancing autonomy and protection in health decisions

Balancing autonomy and protection in health decisions is a complex and delicate task, involving considerations of individual rights, the greater good of society, and ethical principles. Autonomy refers to an individual's right to make decisions about their own health and body, while protection involves safeguarding individuals from harm and promoting public health.

In the context of health decisions, several factors influence the balance between autonomy and protection:

1. Informed Consent: Respect for autonomy requires that individuals have access to accurate and comprehensible information about their health conditions, treatment options, and potential risks and benefits. Informed consent ensures that individuals can make voluntary and well-informed decisions about their health.

2. Capacity to Make Decisions: Autonomy is meaningful when individuals have the cognitive ability to make decisions. When someone lacks the capacity to make decisions due to age, mental illness, or other factors, protection measures, such as appointing a legal guardian, may be necessary.

3. Public Health Considerations: In certain situations, public health interests may take precedence over individual autonomy. For example, during a public health emergency or infectious disease outbreak,

measures such as quarantine or vaccination mandates may be implemented to protect the broader community.

4. Medical Ethics: The principles of medical ethics, such as beneficence (doing good), non-maleficence (avoiding harm), and justice, guide healthcare professionals in balancing individual autonomy with the well-being of their patients.

5. Cultural and Religious Beliefs: Autonomy should be respected within the framework of an individual's cultural and religious beliefs, which may influence their health decisions. Healthcare providers should be sensitive to cultural diversity and tailor care accordingly.

6. Children and Minors: Balancing autonomy and protection is particularly challenging when it comes to children and minors. In such cases, parental or guardian consent is generally required, but there may be exceptions for mature minors or situations involving life-threatening emergencies.

7. End-of-Life Decisions: Discussions about end-of-life care often involve navigating complex ethical and legal issues, such as advance directives, living wills, and the right to refuse treatment.

8. Patient Rights Advocacy: Ensuring that patients are aware of their rights and have access to advocacy services can help protect autonomy in healthcare settings.

To strike the right balance between autonomy and protection, healthcare providers, policymakers, and society at large must consider the unique circumstances of each situation and apply a thoughtful and ethical approach. Respecting autonomy while safeguarding individuals from harm is crucial to upholding human dignity and promoting the overall well-being of individuals and communities.

Confidentiality and disclosure in family health matters

Confidentiality and disclosure in family health matters are critical considerations in the field of healthcare, as they involve the delicate balance between respecting patients' privacy and ensuring the well-being of individuals and their families. Healthcare professionals face ethical and legal obligations regarding the handling of confidential information, especially when it pertains to family health issues. Here are some key aspects related to confidentiality and disclosure in family health matters:

1. Patient Privacy: Healthcare providers are bound by ethical principles and legal regulations to protect the privacy of their patients. This includes keeping medical information confidential and not disclosing any sensitive information to third parties without the patient's explicit consent.

2. Informed Consent: Before sharing any medical information with family members, healthcare providers should obtain the patient's informed consent. Informed consent ensures that the patient is fully aware of the information being shared and the potential consequences of disclosure.

3. Legal Requirements: Laws regarding confidentiality and disclosure vary by jurisdiction. In some cases, healthcare providers may be legally required to report certain health conditions or situations, such as communicable diseases, abuse, or violence, to relevant

authorities.

4. Minor's Privacy: When treating minors, healthcare providers must balance the minor's right to privacy with the parents' or guardians' right to access information about their child's health. The rules governing minor consent and parental involvement in healthcare decisions can differ based on age, jurisdiction, and the nature of the medical condition.

5. Family History: In certain situations, family medical history can be relevant to a patient's diagnosis and treatment. Discussing family history with patients and encouraging them to share relevant information can contribute to better healthcare outcomes.

6. Genetic Information: Genetic testing and family health histories may reveal information that has implications for other family members. Healthcare providers should carefully consider how to approach the sharing of genetic information with patients and their families.

7. End-of-Life Decisions: Discussions about end-of-life care and medical decision-making may involve multiple family members. Healthcare providers should facilitate open communication while respecting the patient's preferences regarding disclosure.

8. Cultural and Religious Considerations: Some cultures and religions may have specific views on confidentiality and disclosure. Healthcare providers should be sensitive to these beliefs and engage in culturally competent communication.

9. Shared Decision-Making: Involving family members in the patient's healthcare decisions can be valuable, but it should be done with the patient's consent and in a manner that respects their autonomy.

Balancing confidentiality and disclosure in family health matters is a complex process that requires careful consideration of the patient's rights, family dynamics, legal requirements, and ethical principles. Healthcare providers must be well-informed about relevant laws and regulations and be guided by ethical principles to ensure that they respect patients' privacy while promoting their health and well-being. Open communication and trust between patients, their families, and healthcare providers are essential for navigating these sensitive issues effectively.

Cultural and religious beliefs versus medical necessities

The clash between cultural and religious beliefs and medical necessities is a complex and sensitive issue that healthcare professionals often encounter in their practice. Balancing these two factors requires understanding and respect for the diverse cultural and religious backgrounds of patients while adhering to the principles of evidence-based medicine and providing the best possible care.

Cultural and Religious Beliefs:

- Cultural and religious beliefs play a significant role in shaping an individual's health beliefs, treatment preferences, and perceptions of illness. These beliefs may impact decisions about medical care, lifestyle choices, and end-of-life decisions.
- Some cultural or religious practices may have implications for medical treatment, such as dietary restrictions, fasting, or specific rituals related to birth and death.
- Healthcare providers should be sensitive to the cultural and religious values of their patients and their families, as these beliefs can influence their overall well-being and response to treatment.

Medical Necessities:

- Medical necessities are based on scientific evidence, clinical guidelines, and best practices that aim to achieve the best possible health outcomes for patients.

- Healthcare providers have an ethical and professional duty to prioritize medical necessities and provide care that is in the best interest of the patient's health and safety.
- In cases where cultural or religious beliefs may interfere with medically necessary treatments, healthcare professionals must carefully balance respecting the patient's beliefs while ensuring that they receive appropriate medical care.

Navigating the Balance:

- Open communication and trust between healthcare providers and patients are essential in navigating the balance between cultural and religious beliefs and medical necessities. Engaging in culturally competent care involves actively listening to the patient, understanding their beliefs, and involving them in shared decision-making.
- Healthcare providers should be aware of and sensitive to potential conflicts between cultural or religious practices and medical treatments. When conflicts arise, an open and respectful dialogue with the patient and their family can help find a solution that aligns with their values while prioritizing their health needs.
- In some cases, seeking the assistance of medical interpreters, cultural liaisons, or religious leaders may facilitate communication and understanding between healthcare providers and patients from different cultural backgrounds.

Ethical Considerations:

- Ethical principles, such as respect for patient autonomy, beneficence, and nonmaleficence, guide healthcare decisions in complex situations involving cultural and religious beliefs.

- When considering medical treatments that may conflict with a patient's cultural or religious beliefs, healthcare providers should explore alternative options that are medically appropriate and align with the patient's values as much as possible.
- In extreme cases where there is a significant risk to the patient's health or life due to a refusal of necessary medical treatment based on cultural or religious beliefs, healthcare providers may need to involve ethics committees or legal authorities to determine the best course of action.

Overall, successfully navigating the intersection of cultural and religious beliefs with medical necessities requires sensitivity, cultural competence, and a patient-centered approach to care. Healthcare providers must strive to find a balance that respects patients' values while upholding the highest standards of medical care and patient safety.

Addressing ethical dilemmas through legal frameworks

Addressing ethical dilemmas through legal frameworks is essential in ensuring that ethical standards are upheld while providing clarity and guidance to healthcare professionals, patients, and their families. Legal frameworks serve as a foundation for defining the rights and responsibilities of all parties involved and provide a structured approach to resolving complex ethical issues. Here are some ways legal frameworks address ethical dilemmas in healthcare:

Informed Consent:

- Legal requirements for informed consent ensure that patients have the right to be fully informed about their medical condition, treatment options, potential risks, benefits, and alternatives.
- Obtaining informed consent is an ethical principle that respects patient autonomy and enables them to make informed decisions about their care.

Patient Privacy and Confidentiality:

- Legal protections of patient privacy and confidentiality are crucial ethical considerations in healthcare.
- Ensuring the privacy of patient information builds trust and safeguards patients' sensitive medical details.

Advance Directives and End-of-Life Care:

- Legal frameworks for advance directives allow

individuals to express their treatment preferences and healthcare decisions in advance, especially in cases where they may lose decision-making capacity.
- These legal documents address ethical dilemmas related to end-of-life care, ensuring that patients' wishes are honored.

Medical Decision-Making for Minors:

- Legal guidelines define the circumstances under which minors can make their medical decisions, consent to treatment, or seek treatment without parental consent.
- Balancing the autonomy and best interests of minors with legal and ethical responsibilities helps healthcare professionals navigate challenging situations.

Ethical Review Committees and Institutional Ethics Boards:

- Many healthcare institutions have ethics review committees or institutional ethics boards that assess and address complex ethical dilemmas in clinical practice, research, and other aspects of healthcare.
- These committees review cases, provide guidance, and ensure that ethical principles are upheld.

Professional Codes of Ethics:

- Legal frameworks often incorporate the codes of ethics of healthcare professionals, which outline the ethical principles and standards they must adhere to in their practice.
- These codes provide guidance for addressing ethical dilemmas while upholding the integrity and professionalism of healthcare providers.

Scope of Practice and Standards of Care:

- Legal frameworks define the scope of practice

for different healthcare professionals and establish standards of care that they must follow.

- Adhering to these legal requirements ensures that ethical practices are maintained within the boundaries of each profession.

Research Ethics:

- Legal and regulatory frameworks govern the conduct of medical research to ensure the protection of human subjects' rights and welfare.
- Ethical considerations in research include informed consent, minimizing risks, and ensuring confidentiality.

By intertwining ethical principles with legal frameworks, healthcare professionals can navigate complex ethical dilemmas more effectively. These legal guidelines provide a structure for decision-making, protect patients' rights, and support healthcare providers in making ethically sound choices in challenging situations. It is crucial for healthcare professionals to have a thorough understanding of these legal frameworks to provide the highest standard of care while upholding ethical principles.

Emerging challenges and opportunities

Emerging challenges and opportunities in family health law are constantly shaping the legal landscape of healthcare. As society and technology evolve, new ethical dilemmas and legal considerations arise. Here are some key challenges and opportunities in family health law:

1. Medical Technology Advancements: With rapid advancements in medical technology, legal frameworks must adapt to address issues related to genetic testing, telemedicine, artificial intelligence in healthcare, and data privacy. Balancing the benefits of technology with patient safety and privacy is a significant challenge.

2. Reproductive Technologies: The increasing use of reproductive technologies, such as in vitro fertilization and preimplantation genetic testing, raises questions about parental rights, surrogacy arrangements, and the legal status of embryos.

3. Health Equity and Access: Ensuring equitable access to quality healthcare for all individuals, regardless of their socioeconomic status, race, or geographic location, is a critical challenge. Family health law must address disparities in healthcare delivery and strive to provide fair and just healthcare outcomes.

4. End-of-Life Care and Medical Aid in Dying: Balancing patient autonomy with end-of-life care decisions and medical aid in dying is an ongoing challenge. Legal frameworks must navigate the sensitive topic of allowing terminally ill patients to make decisions about their care and the availability of medical aid in dying.

5. Pandemic Preparedness and Response: The COVID-19 pandemic highlighted the need for robust legal frameworks to address public health emergencies, quarantine measures, and vaccination distribution. Preparing for future pandemics and ensuring public health while respecting individual rights is a significant opportunity.

6. Mental Health Legislation: Strengthening mental health legislation and addressing mental health issues in family law are critical opportunities. Ensuring access to mental health services, involuntary commitment laws, and safeguarding the rights of individuals with mental health conditions are essential considerations.

7. Ethical Use of Artificial Intelligence: As artificial intelligence and machine learning play a larger role in healthcare decision-making, family health law must address concerns related to patient autonomy, transparency, and the accountability of AI algorithms.

8. Data Privacy and Security: The protection of patient data from cyber threats is an ongoing challenge. Legal frameworks need to ensure that patient information is secure and used responsibly, especially as healthcare becomes increasingly digitized.

9. Global Health Law: With the world becoming more interconnected, legal frameworks for family health law need to address global health challenges, such as infectious disease outbreaks, international health regulations, and cross-border healthcare access.

10. Family Violence and Child Protection: Addressing family violence and ensuring child protection are significant challenges. Legal frameworks should prioritize the safety and well-being of vulnerable individuals within families.

11. Integrating Legal and Ethical Considerations: An opportunity

exists to integrate ethical considerations more comprehensively into family health law to ensure that legal decisions align with the values and needs of patients and families.

12. Education and Training: Providing education and training on family health law to healthcare professionals, legal practitioners, and the public can enhance awareness and understanding of rights and responsibilities in healthcare decision-making.

As family health law continues to evolve, stakeholders must collaborate to develop comprehensive legal frameworks that address these challenges while promoting ethical, compassionate, and patient-centered care. By seizing these opportunities, the field can make significant strides in enhancing the well-being and rights of individuals and families in healthcare settings.

Technological advancements and legal implications

Technological advancements in healthcare have revolutionized the way medical services are delivered and have also brought about new legal implications. Here are some of the key technological advancements and their corresponding legal considerations:

1. Telemedicine and Telehealth: Telemedicine allows patients to receive medical consultations and treatment remotely, often through video conferencing or other digital platforms. Legal considerations include licensure requirements for healthcare providers in different states or countries, patient privacy and data security regulations, and malpractice liability in telemedicine settings.

2. Electronic Health Records (EHRs): The transition from paper-based medical records to EHRs has improved data accessibility and coordination of care. Legal issues related to EHRs include data privacy and security, ensuring patient access to their records, and proper documentation to avoid medical malpractice claims.

3. Artificial Intelligence (AI) in Healthcare: AI is being used for diagnosis, treatment planning, and predicting patient outcomes. Legal implications include issues of liability and accountability in case of AI errors, ensuring transparency in AI decision-making, and data privacy concerns when using patient data to train AI algorithms.

4. Wearable Devices and Remote Monitoring: Wearable devices

and remote monitoring technologies allow continuous tracking of patient health data. Legal considerations include data ownership, patient consent for data collection, and potential challenges in interpreting and using large volumes of real-time health data.

5. Gene Editing and Genetic Technologies: Gene editing technologies like CRISPR have the potential to treat genetic diseases, but they also raise ethical questions about germline editing and genetic manipulation. Legal issues include regulation of gene editing techniques, protecting individuals' genetic information, and addressing potential discrimination based on genetic information.

6. Internet of Things (IoT) in Healthcare: IoT devices, such as medical implants and connected medical equipment, pose cybersecurity risks and privacy concerns. Legal considerations include ensuring the security of IoT devices, safeguarding patient data, and establishing liability in case of IoT-related medical errors.

7. 3D Printing in Healthcare: 3D printing technology is used in medical device manufacturing and creating personalized medical implants. Legal implications include ensuring the safety and quality of 3D-printed medical products, intellectual property rights related to medical device designs, and product liability issues.

8. Virtual Reality (VR) and Augmented Reality (AR): VR and AR have applications in medical training, patient education, and pain management. Legal issues include informed consent for using VR/AR in medical procedures, potential psychological effects, and liability in case of VR-related injuries.

9. Blockchain Technology: Blockchain can enhance data security, interoperability, and transparency in healthcare. Legal considerations include regulatory compliance when using

blockchain for health data, smart contract enforceability, and ensuring patient consent for blockchain-based health records.

10. Robotic Surgery: Robot-assisted surgery offers precision and minimally invasive procedures. Legal implications include liability for surgical errors, informed consent for robotic surgeries, and standardizing training for surgeons using robotic systems.

As technology continues to advance, the legal framework surrounding healthcare must keep pace to address the ethical, privacy, security, and liability concerns that arise. Collaboration between legal experts, healthcare professionals, policymakers, and technology developers is crucial to ensuring that technological innovations are harnessed responsibly and ethically to improve patient care and outcomes while safeguarding patients' rights and well-being.

Integrating family and health law reforms

Integrating family and health law reforms involves harmonizing legal frameworks and policies in both domains to address the complex and interconnected issues that arise at the intersection of family and health matters. Here are some key areas where integration is essential:

1. Reproductive Health and Family Planning: Integrating family and health law reforms can promote access to reproductive health services, including family planning, contraceptives, and fertility treatments. This may involve ensuring that reproductive health services are covered by health insurance and protecting individuals' rights to make decisions about their reproductive choices.

2. Maternal and Child Health: Integrating family and health law can strengthen protections for pregnant women and infants, ensuring access to prenatal care, childbirth services, and postnatal support. Legal reforms may address issues such as maternal health care rights, parental leave, and child custody arrangements.

3. Medical Decision-Making for Minors: Integrating family and health law can provide clarity on medical decision-making for minors, particularly in situations where parents or guardians have differing beliefs about treatment options. Legal reforms can help balance parental rights with the best interests of the child, and establish protocols for obtaining consent for medical procedures.

4. End-of-Life Care and Advance Directives: Integrating family

and health law can facilitate the use of advance directives, living wills, and durable powers of attorney for healthcare decisions. Legal reforms can ensure that individuals' wishes regarding end-of-life care are respected and followed.

5. Child Welfare and Healthcare Access: Integrating family and health law can improve healthcare access for children in foster care or other child welfare systems. Legal reforms may address coordination between child welfare agencies and healthcare providers to ensure continuity of care for vulnerable children.

6. Mental Health and Family Support: Integrating family and health law can enhance mental health services for families, including access to counseling, therapy, and support. Legal reforms can promote family-centered care for individuals dealing with mental health challenges.

7. Medical Privacy and Family Dynamics: Integrating family and health law can navigate the complexities of medical privacy in the context of family relationships. Legal reforms may establish guidelines for sharing medical information among family members while respecting individuals' right to privacy.

8. Domestic Violence and Health Care: Integrating family and health law can strengthen protections for victims of domestic violence and enhance access to medical care and support services. Legal reforms can promote collaboration between healthcare providers and domestic violence advocates.

9. Health Insurance and Family Coverage: Integrating family and health law can address issues related to health insurance coverage for families, including spousal coverage, dependents, and domestic partnerships. Legal reforms may work to ensure equitable access to healthcare benefits for all family structures.

10. Health Disparities and Social Determinants of Health: Integrating family and health law can focus on addressing health disparities that disproportionately affect certain family

populations. Legal reforms may aim to reduce social determinants of health and promote equitable healthcare opportunities for all families.

Integrating family and health law reforms requires a multi-disciplinary approach involving policymakers, legal experts, healthcare professionals, social workers, and community advocates. Collaboration among these stakeholders can lead to comprehensive reforms that better address the needs of families and individuals in the healthcare system, promoting better health outcomes and overall well-being for all members of society.

Vision for a harmonious future at the intersection

In envisioning a harmonious future at the intersection of family and health law, we aspire to create a society where individuals and families are empowered to make informed decisions about their health and well-being, while being supported by comprehensive and equitable legal frameworks. This vision entails:

1. Inclusivity and Respect: The legal system recognizes and respects the diverse range of family structures, cultural backgrounds, and religious beliefs. It ensures that all individuals, regardless of their background, have equal access to healthcare services and can make decisions about their health and family with autonomy and dignity.

2. Holistic Healthcare: Family and health law work in synergy to promote holistic healthcare for all family members. This includes mental health support, preventive care, and access to quality medical services that address both physical and emotional well-being.

3. Empowerment of Individuals and Families: Legal reforms prioritize the empowerment of individuals and families to actively participate in their healthcare journey. This is achieved through robust informed consent processes, comprehensive health education, and accessible resources that enable them to make choices aligned with their values and preferences.

4. Protection of Vulnerable Populations: The legal system safeguards the rights and well-being of vulnerable populations,

including children, the elderly, and individuals with disabilities. It ensures that their voices are heard and their best interests are considered in healthcare and family-related decisions.

5. Collaboration and Coordination: Family and health law stakeholders, including legal professionals, healthcare providers, social workers, and community organizations, collaborate seamlessly to ensure a coordinated approach to healthcare and family support. This collaboration fosters an environment where individuals receive comprehensive care and services tailored to their unique needs.

6. Privacy and Data Security: Legal reforms prioritize the protection of personal health information, ensuring privacy and confidentiality in all healthcare interactions. This builds trust between individuals and healthcare providers and encourages open communication about health concerns.

7. Prevention and Early Intervention: Family and health law embrace prevention and early intervention strategies, with an emphasis on promoting healthy lifestyles and identifying health issues at an early stage. This approach reduces the burden of illness and promotes overall well-being.

8. Ethical Use of Reproductive Technologies: Legal frameworks govern the ethical use of reproductive technologies, ensuring that decisions about fertility treatments, surrogacy, and genetic testing are made responsibly and with consideration for all parties involved.

9. Continuous Learning and Improvement: The legal system adapts to the evolving needs of families and healthcare practices through continuous learning and improvement. Ongoing research and evaluation inform legal reforms that positively impact family health and well-being.

10. Social Support and Community Resilience: Family and health law recognize the importance of social support networks and

community resilience in promoting health and family cohesion. Legal reforms encourage community engagement and support systems that strengthen the well-being of families.

In this harmonious future, family and health law become interconnected elements, working hand in hand to create an environment where individuals and families thrive physically, emotionally, and spiritually. It is a future where the legal system actively supports the health and happiness of all, fostering a society built on compassion, equity, and well-being. By embracing this vision, we pave the way for a brighter future where the intersection of family and health is a source of strength and empowerment for generations to come.

Recapitulation of key insights and themes discussed in the book

Throughout "Family & Health Law: Navigating Ethical Terrain," we have explored a myriad of topics at the intersection of family law and health law. Here's a recap of the key insights and themes discussed in the book:

1. Intersection of Family and Health: We delved into how family dynamics, relationships, and decisions about health are interconnected, highlighting the significance of comprehensive legal frameworks that address the unique challenges at this juncture.

2. Ethical Considerations: Central to our exploration were ethical dilemmas arising from medical treatments, reproductive technologies, end-of-life decisions, and cultural/religious beliefs. We emphasized the importance of balancing autonomy, protection, and respect for the well-being of all individuals involved.

3. Informed Consent and Decision-making: Informed consent emerged as a critical aspect of both family and health law. We examined how empowering individuals and families to make informed decisions can positively impact their health and family well-being.

4. Vulnerable Populations: We explored the legal protections for vulnerable populations, including children, the elderly, and individuals with disabilities, ensuring their rights and best interests are safeguarded.

5. Privacy and Confidentiality: The significance of privacy and confidentiality in healthcare settings was discussed, emphasizing the need for secure handling of health information and fostering trust between patients and healthcare providers.

6. Reproductive Technologies: The legal implications of assisted reproduction, surrogacy, and genetic testing were explored, recognizing the importance of responsible and ethical use of these technologies.

7. End-of-Life Decisions: We examined advance healthcare directives, hospice care, and the right to die, acknowledging the complex legal and ethical considerations surrounding end-of-life decisions.

8. Mental Health and Well-being: Mental health considerations in family law disputes, involuntary commitment, and mental health evaluations were addressed, highlighting the need for sensitivity and support for individuals with mental health concerns.

9. Health Crises and Emergencies: The legal aspects of health crises, quarantine measures, and decision-making during emergencies were discussed, emphasizing the importance of public health and individual rights.

10. Social and Community Support: We acknowledged the role of social support networks and community resilience in promoting family well-being and health outcomes.

Throughout the book, we stressed the importance of a harmonious and comprehensive legal system that upholds ethical principles, empowers individuals and families, and supports their health and well-being. By recognizing the interplay between family dynamics and health decisions, we envision a future where legal frameworks promote compassion, equity, and the health and happiness of all individuals and families.

A call to action for promoting a just and compassionate family and health law system

In "Family Matters: Navigating the Intersection of Family & Health Law," we have delved into the complex and intertwined realms of family and health, exploring the ethical considerations, legal complexities, and the profound impact on individuals' lives. As we conclude this enlightening journey, we issue a heartfelt call to action for promoting a just and compassionate family and health law system that fosters the well-being of all individuals and communities.

1. Promote Ethical Practices: Encourage ethical decision-making by legal professionals, healthcare providers, and individuals involved in family and health-related matters. Uphold the principles of autonomy, beneficence, and non-maleficence, ensuring that decisions are made with compassion and sensitivity to the diverse needs and values of families.

2. Empower Informed Decision-making: Advocate for accessible information and education on legal and health matters, empowering individuals and families to make informed choices that align with their values and circumstances. Ensure that individuals fully understand their rights and options.

3. Strengthen Support Networks: Foster strong social support networks and community resources to assist families and individuals during challenging times. Collaboration between legal, medical, and community organizations can enhance the overall well-being of

families facing complex situations.

4. Protect Vulnerable Populations: Develop and enforce legal protections for vulnerable populations, including children, the elderly, individuals with disabilities, and those facing mental health challenges. Safeguard their rights, autonomy, and dignity throughout legal and health processes.

5. Advance Research and Policy: Encourage research and policy development to address emerging challenges at the intersection of family and health. Advocate for progressive laws that promote inclusivity, diversity, and fairness in family and health-related matters.

6. Foster Open Dialogue: Promote open and respectful dialogue among legal professionals, healthcare providers, policymakers, and communities to address ethical dilemmas and complex legal issues effectively. Collaboration and exchange of knowledge can lead to more holistic solutions.

7. Embrace Cultural Competency: Encourage cultural competence and sensitivity in the legal and healthcare fields. Recognize and respect diverse cultural and religious beliefs, ensuring that the law is inclusive and respectful of everyone's values and practices.

8. Support Mental Health Services: Advocate for accessible and compassionate mental health services that promote early intervention and support for individuals and families facing mental health challenges. Addressing mental health concerns can significantly impact overall well-being.

9. Promote Community Awareness: Raise public awareness of family and health law matters and their implications on individuals' lives. Educate the public about their legal rights and resources available to them.

10.   Be Agents of Change: As legal professionals, healthcare providers, policymakers, and individuals, we

can all play a role in advocating for a just and compassionate family and health law system. Let us commit to fostering positive change and creating a more empathetic and supportive environment for families and individuals navigating these complex domains.

By embracing these principles and taking meaningful actions, we can collectively contribute to a family and health law system that embodies justice, compassion, and inclusivity, ultimately enriching the lives of individuals and communities worldwide. Together, let us build a more equitable and caring world for all.

www.ingramcontent.com/pod-product-compliance
Lightning Source LLC
Chambersburg PA
CBHW062316290526
45794CB00005B/1823